Dear Reader:

The book you are about to read is the latest bestseller from the St. Martin's True Crime Library, the imprint *The New York Times* calls "the leader in true crime!" Each month, we offer you a fascinating account of the latest, most sensational crime that has captured the national attention. St. Martin's is the publisher of bestselling true crime author and crime journalist Kieran Crowley, who explores the dark, deadly links between a prominent Manhattan surgeon and the disappearance of his wife fifteen years earlier in THE SURGEON'S WIFE. Suzy Spencer's BREAKING POINT guides readers through the tortuous twists and turns in the case of Andrea Yates, the Houston mother who drowned her five young children in the family's bathtub. In Edgar Award-nominated DARK DREAMS, legendary FBI profiler Roy Hazelwood and bestselling crime author Stephen G. Michaud shine light on the inner workings of America's most violent and depraved murderers. In the book you now hold, DESIRE TURNED DEADLY, author Kevin F. McMurray looks into a case of teenage love that ended in tragedy.

St. Martin's True Crime Library gives you the stories behind the headlines. Our authors take you right to the scene of the crime and into the minds of the most notorious murderers to show you what really makes them tick. St. Martin's True Crime Library paperbacks are better than the most terrifying thriller, because it's all true! The next time you want a crackling good read, make sure it's got the St. Martin's True Crime Library logo on the spine—you'll be up all night!

Charles E. Spicer, Jr.
Executive Editor, St. Martin's True Crime Library

St. Martin's Paperbacks True Crime Library Titles
by Kevin F. McMurray

A Family Cursed

If You Really Loved Me

DESIRE TURNED DEADLY

*The True Story of a Beautiful Girl, Her Teenage Sweetheart,
and the Love that Ended in Murder*

Kevin F. McMurray

St. Martin's Paperbacks

Contents

Contents

DESIRE TURNED
DEADLY

Prologue

Nov. 13, 2005

It was promising to be another chilly, monochromatic mid-November morning, perhaps a touch warmer than usual, when the young girl cautiously approached the two-floor frame house that sat on a slight rise above the quiet, residential street. The weather in southeastern Pennsylvania had settled into the stark days of autumn that would inexorably give way to the long frozen lock of winter. But this morning it was the colorful, vibrant days of summer that warmed the young girl's heart: the flirtatious friendship that she'd nurtured had blossomed into the torrid affair that it now was. The coming months of winter held only the promise of better things for the young girl, who was hopelessly immersed in a first love.

Even though there was no frost, the ground underfoot was as hard as concrete as the pretty, petite blonde paused to cast a furtive glance over her shoulder at the house across the street. The family who lived in the ranch-style home was not likely to be up at this ungodly time of morning. The predawn hours, especially on Sundays, were deathly quiet in the quaint community of Lititz, so she had no worry about being seen. But she knew the neighbors would not hesitate to inform her parents that their 14-year-old daughter had been sneaking into the house at 5 AM on the Sabbath. She couldn't be too careful, but, as she stole glances to her left and right in search of human movement, her mind kept wandering back to David and their delicious lovemaking in the wee hours of the morning.

She stepped onto the first-floor porch, praying that the boards underfoot would not groan with her slight weight, giving notice of her presence. She peered into the window and scanned the darkened room. Nothing. She breathed a sigh of relief as she reached for the window frame.

Kara Beth Borden grasped the window and lifted it ever so slowly. She congratulated herself for remembering to unlock it before slipping out of the house hours before. It was eerily silent as the sash slid up noiselessly in its frame. Kara was thankful that the boisterous, early morning songbirds had already fled for the warmer climates of the southlands. Other than her own fluid efforts, no sounds would invade the quiet household.

Kara had often thought about what her strict, overly protective parents would do if they found her out. Being a devoutly religious couple, there surely would be words of how eternal damnation awaited her for her sinful ways. Pleasures of the flesh were particularly frowned upon in the Borden home. She smiled to herself at the thought of how they would react to the knowledge that their innocent young daughter was now a woman, eagerly engaged in a sexual relationship with a handsome, virile young man. David and she often talked about it when they were in each other's arms after their vigorous lovemaking. But soon she would not have to worry about being caught; in just a week's time, she and David would be fleeing for their new life together.

At first, their plans for running off were out of necessity, since her period was late and a pregnancy would dictate an escape from her sheltered childhood. But that had been a false alarm. Still, the thought of their getaway was too tempting to let go, pregnant or not. Being together 24/7 was something the two constantly talked about. Why should they waste their youth apart? Their love was way too intense for that.

She was constantly warned by her friends, particularly Kayla Jeffries, who'd known David for what seemed like forever, that Kara was too young and David had a "history."

Kara knew all about his romantic dalliances. He had been honest with her about them. David had assured her that they'd all been foolish affairs of a young, horny teenager.

She had convinced herself that David would be a good husband and provider. Besides being handsome, he was strong, smart and ambitious. How could she do better?

The window was up now as far as she dared raise it. She lifted her right leg and slid it over the sill. With a little hop of her left foot, she was straddling the sill. She ducked her head under the raised window and silently slipped into the room that she was beginning to see, now that her eyes had adjusted to the dark.

Turning back to the window, she gingerly lowered it, then turned toward the staircase that led to her bedroom. But there, blocking her path, was her mother. Standing in the alcove only a couple of paces from Kara, arms folded, she stared at her daughter with fierce, angry eyes. Kara froze in her tracks; her lips shut tight, her breath stilled. Her heart immediately started to race.

Kara managed to summon her voice and blurt out, "Mother!" It was more an exclamation of shock than of puzzlement, which she lamely tried to feign.

Pressing her right hand to her breast, she said, "You scared me!" That at least was the truth.

"Where were you, young lady?" her mother demanded in a flat voice edged with a righteous rage. She was rubbing her eyes clear of what little sleep she'd gotten while napping on the living room couch anticipating the arrival of her wayward daughter.

Kara stuttered before finally mumbling that she was just seeing a girlfriend who'd needed to meet with her. Pausing in her impromptu explanation, Kara regained some of her shaken composure. She tried to further obfuscate the matter by explaining that she'd just *had* to go, and she knew they would never allow her, had she asked for permission.

"Well, you got that right!" her mother said with a stifled laugh. Just then, Kara saw her father step into the room from the stairs that led to the bedrooms on the second floor. He was staring intently at Kara as he tied the sash of his robe around his midriff. Kara took a quick, deep breath. She now knew her worst nightmare was being realized. She had finally been found out.

For the next fifteen minutes her parents tag-teamed her with question after question. They were unrelenting, making her trip over her words and forcing Kara to alter her story along the way. It seemed that every sentence they uttered started with, "But you just said . . ."

Even though Kara feared her 50-year-old parents, she could feel her own anger well in her throat, making her lock her teeth and narrow her eyes. Her face flushed with rage. They couldn't treat her like a child forever! She stood silently and watched her parents cast more accusations in her direction and demand answers for a few more moments, until she hollered out, "YES, YES, YESSSS!" dragging out the last word in exasperation, with tears of frustration pooling in her eyes. Both of her parents fell immediately silent. Their eyes widened and the color noticeably drained from her dad's face, leaving him with the pallor of an eggshell.

Just then, almost as if on cue, Kara's cell phone chimed notice of the arrival of a text message. The timing of the call almost made the teenager burst into laughter. Her dad let out an audible snort, while her mother shot a conspiratorial look at her husband. Kara thought for a moment about ignoring it, but quickly figured that doing so would only suggest that she was hiding something. She flipped open her cell and stared at the message on the screen.

A few seconds passed before her father, sensing the potential importance of what the LCD display screen said, snatched the phone from his daughter, leaving her speechless, her hand still suspended outward. Mr. Borden glared at the illuminated screen, before he raised his head slowly and finally said, "So it is that Ludwig boy."

There. It had finally been said. It was David Ludwig she had been seeing—and apparently sleeping with. "Fuck it!" she thought. "I'm glad it's out!"

Before her parents could get another word in, Kara, as calmly and defiantly as she could, stated, "We're in love and we're going to get married!"

Her mother raised both of her hands to her ears in an unintentional mimicry of Edvard Munch's *The Scream*. Her father laughed in a staccato burst before finally saying in a decibel level just below a holler, "Like hell you will!"

Both mother and daughter turned to stare at the head of their household in bewildered shock, for the ultra-religious Michael Borden had never uttered such a profanity before in their presence.

It was about two hours, several exchanges of text messages and a couple of voice connections later that David Ludwig walked along the driveway of his downtown Lititz home and piled the load of weaponry he had assembled on the front passenger seat of his father's red 1998 VW Jetta. The tall brown-haired teenager moved with a sense of purpose. His jaw was set and he went about his tasks with an economy of movement. He felt like a soldier preparing for battle.

Kara's father had requested that he come over so they could have a discussion about David's relationship with his daughter. Kara had told him she'd been caught sneaking back into the house and had confessed to the nature of their friendship. Things had gotten ugly. Kara's parents were on the warpath.

Behind the wheel of the car, David double-checked the chamber of his Glock 17 and the loaded magazine that slid into the handle of the .40-caliber semiautomatic handgun. It was the weapon of choice in many police departments across the country. The model 17 was reliable, lightweight and extremely deadly. Satisfied with his rushed preparations, he turned the ignition key, gunned the gas, then slipped it into gear and backed out of the driveway.

At the corner of West Orange Street, he turned right on South Broad and headed for the Borden home on Royal Drive via Owl Hill Road, three miles distant, about five minutes by car on this quiet Sunday morning. It was the second time this morning that he had made this run. Just a few short hours ago, he had driven this route when dropping off Kara after her early morning visit to his room.

While driving, David went through all the possible scenarios he might encounter. Looking at his stash of weaponry on the seat beside him, he knew he was prepared for all of them. It would be up to Kara's dad how things turned out.

David parked on the street a couple of doors down from the Borden residence. He did not want to be seen from the house as he collected his weapons and secured them in the old towel he had brought along.

Just before opening his door and exiting the Jetta, David checked the Glock one more time. There was a cartridge chambered. Releasing the semiautomatic pistol's action, he pulled up his shirt and stuffed the Glock down the waistband of his pants. He patted the pistol with the palm of his hand, which gave him a warm feeling of power.

The pistol had a low profile. Nobody, even if they stared, would be able to make out the gun under his shirt.

Mr. Borden answered David's raps on the front door. There was to be no greeting. His eyes immediately fell on the bundle David carried under his right arm.

"You can leave that on the porch."

David complied and lowered the bundled weapons onto the porch floor, and quickly stood up to face Kara's dad again. Without a word, Michael Borden stepped back and opened the door and motioned to David to enter, which he did without hesitation. David stepped aside and waited for Mr. Borden to shut the door and lead the way to wherever they were going.

With Michael Borden's back to him, and shielded from the rest of the room, David patted the Glock in his waistband again for a little reassurance. He was then led to the living area and took a seat on the couch. Michael Borden sat at the other end.

David nodded to Mrs. Borden, who was seated in a recliner chair just a few feet away. She watched David with a sour look on her face, as if she had just swallowed something bitter.

The "conversation" went pretty much the way he'd thought it would. There was, of course, plenty of moralizing about the sinfulness of the relationship. That was to be expected of the devout Bordens. They wanted it to end immediately. Kara would not be allowed to see him, and he was not to try to contact her. The consequences for his failure to abide by their dictums would be his arrest. Kara was only 14 years old, a minor in the eyes of the Commonwealth of Pennsylvania. David was legally an adult at 18 years of age, and because of the nature of his relationship with their daughter, a jail cell awaited him if they chose to bring it to the attention of the authorities. That, however, would only happen if he persisted in seeing Kara. David would also have to tell his parents what had happened if he did not abide by the wishes of the Bordens.

David had been in the home for no more than forty-five minutes when Mr. Borden stood abruptly and announced that their discussion was over, and that it was time for David to leave. Mr. Borden gestured for David to follow him. Michael Borden headed for the door. David Ludwig now knew what he had to do.

As Mr. Borden reached for the doorknob, David pulled up his shirt, exposing the gun handle. In one fluid motion the Glock was in his hand and pointed at the back of Michael Borden's head.

ONE

Lititz, PA

Lititz, Pennsylvania, is a town of 9,000 situated amidst the rolling farmlands of Lancaster County, the very heart of Pennsylvania Dutch country, in the southern tier of the Keystone State, 80 miles west of Philadelphia. Lititz is one of the satellite communities that radiate out like spokes from the hub—the city of Lancaster. With a population of approximately 56,000, Lancaster lays claim to being the oldest inland city in the United States, having been settled in 1718. The city also boasts of having been the capital of the newly birthed United States of America for exactly one day when the encroaching British troops forced the Continental Congress to convene there after abandoning the colonial capital of Philadelphia in 1777.

The simple God-fearing Amish, Moravian and Mennonite people settled here beginning in the 17th century and gave the area its flavor and color. They had come to arable lands after shaking off the yokes of religious persecution in their ancestral homes in Central Europe, and had begun to till the fertile soil and freely practice their fundamental religious beliefs.

Today many of "the Plain People" are still seen about, simply dressed in their 19th century–inspired garb, riding in horse-drawn buggies eschewing the modern day amenities which most of us take for granted. The forty-five churches within its environs form a testament to the religious bent of the small, quaint village.

Steeped in a rich history, Lancaster County's seemingly omnipresent colonial-era cemeteries, their time- and weather-worn tombstones marking battle casualties, attest to the capacious amount of patriots' blood spilled during the Revolutionary War. It is hard to square that war of independence, which was fought with such ferocity in these parts, with the almost tangible tranquility of the place today. Lititz, in the north-central part of the county, epitomizes that peaceful atmosphere.

The streets of downtown Lititz are lined with towering, broad oaks and maples that shadow the century-old homes whose wood-frame porches, complete with swings, crowd the narrow sidewalks. The village is also home to the Sturgis pretzel house, which bills itself as America's first pretzel bakery.

The paucity of violent crimes further buttresses its well-deserved reputation as a safe and amicable place to raise a family. That reputation was spoiled during the first couple of weeks of November 2005.

Detective Eric Zimmerman is, as he says, a "local boy" from Ephrata, just 7 miles from the Warwick Township Police Department headquarters. The township—population 15,000—surrounds the village of Lititz, which has its own small borough police force.

A boyish-looking 37 years of age, Zimmerman had been a cop with the department ever since his hitch was up with the Marine Corps in 1988.

Warwick Township averages just one homicide every ten years, but things had been shaken up with a November 8 gunshot wounding of Lititz Borough Officer Jevon Miller, who was trying to make an arrest of a wanted petty criminal, Daniel Faust. After shooting Miller—the first cop shooting in the history of both police departments—Faust fled the scene and was hunted down seven hours later in the southern end of Lancaster County by a consortium of local police department officers and the Pennsylvania State Police. Faust was killed in the shootout. He had been wanted on a misdemeanor charge.

The community was still abuzz, and some cops were still on leave as a result of the Faust shooting when the sun broke through the dark early morning hours of Sunday, November 13.

At 7:58 AM a 911 call came into the Warwick Township Police Department notifying the police that shots had been fired. The caller was a neighbor of the household where the gunfire seemed to have emanated from. The neighbor identified the house in question as being 15 Royal Drive, less than two miles from police headquarters.

At 8:03 AM, Sergeant Richard Groff and Officer Samuel DaBella arrived at the house on Royal Drive. Establishing a perimeter, Sergeant Groff walked around to the back of the house with his handgun drawn. Just then a young blonde teenage girl bolted from the rear door and ran off in the direction of a neighbor's house. Groff ran after her, and quickly caught up just as she got to the house directly behind the suspect residence. Inside the neighbor's house, the police sergeant learned that she was Katelyn Borden, 15, and she lived with her family in the home she just had fled. In a panic-stricken voice, she managed to blurt out that her parents had been shot.

Groff immediately got on his handheld radio and requested backup, more police units to assist in securing the Borden home. He went back to get more information from the shaken teenager on what had happened.

Katelyn told the 31-year veteran cop that her sister Kara's boyfriend, 18-year-old David Ludwig, had come over to their house that morning to speak with her parents. They had argued and Ludwig wound up shooting her parents.

Katelyn related that after she saw her father shot, she had run up the stairs. Then she'd heard another shot. She quickly hid in her second-floor bathroom, locked herself in, and huddled in the bathtub, keeping as quiet as she possibly could, trying to stifle her heavy, adrenaline-fueled breathing. She heard David Ludwig scream for her younger sister Kara, and listened as the shooter walked around the house, downstairs and up, calling out her sister's name. Then everything got quiet. Ludwig had exited the house. After what seemed an eternity, Katelyn had emerged from her hiding place. Then she ran to the neighbor's, where Groff had caught up with her.

Things hadn't quite returned to normal for the Lititz and Warwick police departments since the Faust gunfight a week prior. Officers were still on administrative leave pending the obligatory departmental investigations, since they had fired their weapons in the shootout with the fugitive Faust. Consequently both departments were short-handed when Eric Zimmerman was woken by his wife at around 8 AM that unseasonably warm Sunday morning.

Zimmerman was groggy with fatigue, since his twelve-hour on-duty shift had finished barely five hours before. His concerned wife had heard the neighborhood buzz about some police activity over in Warwick Township just outside the Lititz borough line. Their son was staying over at a buddy's house in that neighborhood. Zimmerman picked up his portable police-issue radio and flicked on the switch. Through the noisy chatter his trained ear was able to decipher that something was indeed amiss near his department's offices. A cordoned-off perimeter was being set up.

"You better iron me a shirt," he told his wife as he rolled out of bed to get ready to deal with yet another shooting incident. Sure enough, his department-issue cell phone rang five minutes later.

The call was from Lancaster County Communications. They had received a call from Sergeant Richard Groff of Warwick Township Police Department that there had been a shooting and they needed manpower to secure the scene. Zimmerman's name had been taken from "the list."

The list was the brainchild of Detective Joe Geesey and Assistant District Attorney Craig Stedman, both with the Lancaster County District Attorney's Office in the city of Lancaster. Just seven years old, the innovative list was attracting the attention of police departments around the state and the nation.

Lancaster County has thirty-one independent police departments that range in size from just two-member forces up to 150 in Lancaster proper. Most are not equipped to handle major felonies by themselves, so the Major Crimes Forensic Unit (MCFU) was born.

Detective Geesey and ADA Stedman put together a protocol and got all the county department chiefs to agree to it, and also supply names of seasoned investigators who could be called on in the event of a major felony that could not be handled by one municipal department. With MCFU, according to coordinator Geesey, "we can bring a lot of people and resources to a case right away." Lieutenant Ed Tobin, in charge of criminal investigations for Warwick Township, said the MCFU "makes a small department a big department real fast."

Geesey, or whoever has the communications duty, can make the call to an investigator without getting permission from his chief, and the investigator's department pays his overtime. Manheim Township, with just two full-time officers, had originally balked at the idea, but eventually signed on. They were glad they did. Not long after the protocol was instituted, Manheim PD was hit with two homicides in the course of two weeks. MCFU poured in detectives and crime-scene experts, and rescued the investigations. Manheim saved precious time and a lot of money, and got the perpetrators behind bars.

MCFU protocol in a case calls for the chief law enforcement officer of the jurisdiction where the crime happened to designate the chief investigator from his department and the county detective assigns an investigator. The two officers become the chief co-investigators, and assign duties and manage the case. The shootings at 15 Royal Drive would put the MCFU to the toughest test yet of its effectiveness.

Township Police Chief Richard Garipoli, upon learning of the shootings that Sunday morning, immediately alerted the MCFU. Minutes later the call went out to Detective Zimmerman. The mobile command unit for the county was dispatched to the scene. The unit was a truck with communications capability, interview areas and staffing resources. It was located one street over on Kings Cross Road, parallel to the crime scene, 200 to 300 yards from the residence.

Zimmerman quickly learned that the Strategic Emergency Response Team (SERT) was on its way to the shooting scene. Zimmerman knew what that meant: the shooter was believed to still be in the area, and the heavy artillery was there to contain him, and to provide hostage negotiators. Two children were also in the unit and being questioned by detectives. They were Katelyn and David Borden, residents of 15 Royal Drive. Zimmerman was given the task of calling residents of the street to gather intelligence for the assembled police force.

Chief Garipoli selected his most senior detective, Lieutenant Detective Ed Tobin, a twenty-one-year veteran of the township police, to investigate the case. The affable, athletic 48-year-old is infinitely more comfortable in sweats than a coat and tie.

Originally from Hoboken, New Jersey, Tobin moved to Pennsylvania to pursue a dream of working in law enforcement. After completing his course of study at the State Police Academy in Hershey, he made friends with some fellow cadets from Lancaster County and asked them to keep in touch so if anything opened up in their populous, well-to-do county, they'd be sure to give him the heads-up. They did. In 1984 he became a patrolman for Warwick Township, and by 1988, he'd made detective.

Tobin was a friend of Detective Joe Geesey, and they had worked well together in past investigations. At 72 years of age, Geesey was not yet ready for retirement. Small in stature but solid from his years as a wrestler and a wrestling coach, Geesey could more than hold his own in a physical struggle with men half his age. The only thing that gave away his years was a receding scalp of silver-gray hair and an air of experience that comes from being a cop and dealing with the dregs of society for nearly half a century. Despite the world-weariness that a lifetime of crime-fighting can mete out, Joe Geesey is a friendly, polite man with a warm smile and an intuitive mind. He also loves his work.

On that Sunday morning, Ed Tobin had risen early and was doing his daily exercises when he got a call from Chief Garipoli at around 8 AM. Garipoli told his top investigator that they thought there had been a shooting, but didn't know what the circumstances were. Conferring for a few moments, the two men decided Tobin would be on call until more was learned. Twenty minutes later, Garipoli called back and confirmed that there had been a shooting up on Royal Drive and he wanted Tobin to respond.

Between 9 and 9:30 AM, Ed Tobin arrived at the MCFU command center truck on Kings Cross Road.

Several minutes later Detective Joe Geesey and the district attorney for Lancaster County, Donald Totaro, arrived. All agreed that Geesey would be the case manager and Tobin the lead investigator.

Both seasoned detectives knew the first twenty-four hours were the most important in any criminal investigation, so they immediately pored over the MCFU list, culling from it as many investigators as they could get to the crime scene as quickly as possible. The calls went out.

Next the prime focus was for the police to identify the victims, if any, and compile a suspect list. In the meantime the SERT team was approaching the number 15 house on Royal Drive.

TWO

SERT Intervention

Brian Hicks, his wife, Donna, and their teenage son live directly across the street from the Borden residence. Brian was still in bed when he heard the two gunshots shatter the morning peace. Their bedroom, on the first floor of their ranch-style home, looked out on the Borden house, which sits on a grassy knoll. Although startled by the early morning blasts, Brian didn't give it too much thought until he heard the wail of police sirens.

Donna Hicks peeked out the bedroom window and saw a police squad car parked sideways in the street in front of their neighbors' house. She became alarmed when she saw the officer outside of his vehicle with his gun drawn. Looking down Royal Drive, she saw more cop cars blocking the street at the entrance to Rudy Dam Road with their lights flashing. Something was seriously wrong.

It wasn't long before their backyard was, said Brian, "crawling with cops." An officer in combat gear banged on their rear door and informed the frightened couple that shots had been fired at the Borden residence, and Mr. Borden was "down" and the shooter may still be in the house. They were told by the officers to keep away from their windows. Minutes later Police Chief Garipoli was at their rear door requesting that the couple and their son accompany him to the command center a block away. They quickly piled into the unmarked car and were sped away. Other nearby neighbors' homes were also cleared, leaving the mid-block area deserted and ready for the next police operation.

Lieutenant Jason Zahm of the Lancaster City Bureau of Police is the leader of the county's SERT. Of average height and weight, and with no obvious physical attributes that would draw attention to him, Zahm had the reputation among his peers as a straightforward kind of a cop who takes his job very seriously and is very professional. His perfunctory, military manner spoke volumes for the man. Geesey and Tobin knew that with Zahm leading it, the SERT team would proceed efficiently, safely and by the book.

SERT operates much like MCFU and draws its members from fourteen police departments in Lancaster County. SERT, also known as a SWAT team, is comprised of sixty-four men; forty of them are tactical officers, ten are medics, ten are negotiators, and there are also three doctors and one chaplain. The medics are professional nurses and doctors, not police officers. These paramedics train with the team and are an integral part of it, but they do not get involved in any police action, their job being solely to administer to the wounded.

At 8:30 AM Lieutenant Zahm received a phone call from Lancaster County-Wide Communications and was apprised of the situation over in Warwick Township on Royal Drive. Zahm then had county-wide alert service activate the paging system. Within five minutes all members of the team were notified of a possible shooter holding hostages. Within forty minutes, the team was assembled at the shooting scene's mobile unit parked on Kings Cross Road, one block over from Royal Drive. The team members had all their necessary gear and weapons with them, as required, sparing them the need to go to their department headquarters (HQ) or a central station.

On Kings Cross Road at about 9:15 AM, Zahm met with Chief Garipoli, who filled him in on the latest information they'd been able to gather. The first action the SERT took was the evacuation of homes adjacent to 15 Royal Drive; five people were removed from number 7. Two squads were sent to neighbors' homes to collect the two Borden children, who had sought protection there, and where they had made the 911 calls.

Lieutenant Zahm had to assume the shooter was still in the house, since one of the first police officers on the scene believed he had seen an armed figure moving about inside. The SERT negotiators, all detectives, began to act as information gatherers, collecting details from the questioning of the two Borden teenagers and any witnesses who had stepped forward. Zahm interviewed young David Borden himself. David told him there had been an argument, that his father had been shot and that he had heard another shot as he'd run upstairs with his sister.

David related to Zahm that his father was lying in the vestibule area and his mother had been in the living area. Zahm assumed that 50-year-old Michael

Borden was dead, but there was no accountability for 50-year-old Cathryn Borden, 14-year-old Kara and the shooter. Zahm put four marksmen on standby, two at the back of the house, two in the front, using the cover that was available to them outside the neighbors' homes. If they had the window of opportunity with the shooter, Zahm had told them, "Take it!"

Next the commanding officer prepared his entry team to storm the attractive two-floor home on the rise set some twenty-five yards back from the street. The team was split in two: six men were to enter through the back door, and eight through the front door. The team members were dressed in their olive drab Battle Dress Uniforms (BDU), high-ankle boots, ballistic helmets, and a ballistic level-3A vest (designed to stop a 9mm bullet). Every officer was armed with a .40-caliber Glock semiautomatic pistol and, as their primary weapon, either an NP-9 submachine gun that fires a .40-caliber pistol round or an M-4 carbine, a chopped-down version of the military's M-16 standard issue semiautomatic rifle. The chemical munitions officers carried tear gas, pepper gas shot and dispersionary grenades (flash-bang non-lethal weapons).

Zahm made the tactical decision to fire tear gas into the Borden home prior to entry into the house. He did not take the use of tear gas lightly, knowing that it was often a detriment to the effectiveness of the team during a hostage rescue. Several tear gas canisters were fired through the windows of the front of the house and one was shot through the side door in the garage. The team waited a couple of minutes for the gas to spread. Then flash-bang grenades were lobbed in and the officers stormed the house.

The concept behind a SERT hostage rescue is not to go in and hunt for the "bad guy," but to get in, get the hostages and get out. Once that is done, the team is left with a lone gunman with no leverage, a simple barricade situation, which, says Zahm, "is easy to deal with."

The house was "cleared" in less than thirty seconds. Mr. Borden was found, as gathered information had told them, just inside the front door. Mrs. Borden was located in the living area. Both were pronounced dead by team medics. The team quickly withdrew from the house after determining that no one alive was left in the house. All entrances were secured by the officers, and the premises were turned over to the investigation team.

Afterwards it was learned that a jogger who had been running along Royal Drive had heard the shots and seen the shooter exit the house and run around back before leaving the scene in his car. It was the kind of information that Zahm wished he'd had at the beginning, but, he said, "It doesn't always come together."

In their effort to locate David and Kara, a small detachment of the SERT was sent to David Ludwig's house in Lititz in support of Lititz Borough police to hunt for him. The officers received voluntary consent from a surprised Mr. Ludwig for a cursory search for his son. During the quick operation, SERT members clearly could see into the upper level of the residence. In plain view they spied gun cases and computer systems. The officers also saw several firearms on the main level of the house.

SERT officers had to force open a locked door to

what turned out to be the "hobby room." Measuring eight by ten feet, it was where most of the family's gun collection was kept. There was a small arsenal inside the room.

A door that led downstairs to a sublevel basement revealed a 12' × 12' cement block bunker with various alternate light sources, food rations, first-aid kits and other items that would make a prolonged stay in the underground habitat feasible.

The leaked discovery of the bunker would fire the public's imagination. Detectives and the media would find themselves peeking into the closely guarded world of homeschooling, religious fundamentalism, doomsday adherents and the Internet world of teenaged voyeurs.

THREE

Crime Scene

After the Borden house was cleared by SERT, Detective Eric Zimmerman, Lieutenant Ed Tobin and Curtis Ochs did their walk-through of the residence. Prior to entry, all three donned their protective clothing, booties and latex gloves so they wouldn't contaminate the crime scene.

Mr. Borden's body was encountered immediately as they entered the front door. There was a small pool of blood under his head, since he was lying on the exit wound. The neat entry wound was clearly visible to the three investigators. A bullet hole in the door frame, just about eye level, confirmed their belief that Mr. Borden had been shot clean through the head. They then proceeded a few steps down the hallway to the living area, where they saw Mrs. Borden still sitting, but slumped over, in the recliner chair. Zimmerman could see the entry wound in her right temple.

By police standards, the crime scene was surprisingly clean. There was not a lot of blood spilt, no signs of struggle and apparently no violent disruption in the home. As a matter of fact, what damage there was had been mostly created by the SERT when they fired tear gas through the front glass windows and stormed the house in their military-like operation.

County Deputy Coroners Terry Conrad and Rachael Thomas arrived at the house and made the official death pronouncement of Michael and Cathryn Borden at 1:21 PM.

Zimmerman checked the telephone answering machine for messages. Nothing. Next they went upstairs, where they found nothing out of the ordinary. Once the walk-through was completed, Zimmerman and Tobin exited the house, as policy dictated, and let Ochs and his men do their jobs: dusting for latent fingerprints, measuring distances, collecting and bagging material evidence and drawing views of the crime scene that are later developed into charts and used at trial. Like SERT and the MCFU team from the crime-scene detectives were drawn from around the county: Chris Kelly, from Lititz PD, Eric Schmitt, and Kenny Lockhart, from Ephrata PD, and Scott Eelman, from East Lampeter Township PD.

Before police operations were relocated to Warwick Township Police Department headquarters, Detective Tobin interviewed 15-year-old Katelyn Borden. Like her younger sister Kara, Katelyn was slim and petite, naturally blonde and very pretty.

According to Warwick detectives, she was "very, very afraid and shaking . . . trying to take it all in even though she was in a state of shock." Katelyn feared for her brother and missing sister Kara, but she knew the information that she could give Lieutenant Tobin was very important; she tried to control her emotions so she was clear in what she told him.

Katelyn said that her dad and David Ludwig, her sister's boyfriend, had had a serious but civil conversation. Tobin figured that Katelyn had known about her sister's relationship with Ludwig, since only a year separated them and they must have shared secrets—plus, she had immediately identified the gunman as Kara's boyfriend. He looked at the scared young girl and realized she would probably be his best witness to the crimes. He had to be careful how he handled her if she were to be a credible eyewitness in court proceedings that were sure to come.

Katelyn told him she had watched as David Ludwig pulled a handgun from his waistband and shot her unsuspecting father in the back of the head as he was showing him to the door. She related how she had immediately run upstairs after watching Ludwig shoot her father. Then she'd heard the second shot. She knew the crazed 18-year-old had just shot her mother. Katelyn ran to a second-floor bathroom and locked herself in, convinced that Ludwig would come looking for her. She remembers being so scared that she couldn't think straight.

Despite seeing her father shot, knowing her mom had been shot moments later, and fearing for her sister's life, young Katelyn was an "excellent witness" to the crimes, Tobin said. As it would turn out, she would prove to be the authorities' best.

When the house at 15 Royal Drive had been cordoned off, police operations reassembled back at the Warwick Township police headquarters. Detective Kerry Sweigart was given the task of re-interviewing Katelyn to fill in the blanks of Tobin's initial interview.

Sweigart, of East Cocalico Township Police Department, a member of Lancaster County's MCFU, was a muscularly built 40-year-old. He had a reputation, according to one fellow officer, for being "a very outgoing, personable and comfortable guy to be around." Lead Case Detective Ed Tobin considered him to be "a very good interviewer" and said that as a criminal investigator, Sweigart "was not afraid to step forward for critical assignments and interviews." Both Tobin and Joe Geesey had developed a hefty amount of respect for the eighteen-year veteran through the years and the many cases they'd worked on together.

Sweigart had been off duty Sunday, having been called in by the MCFU for the emergency. He'd gotten the word on his cell phone when he, a divorced father, was dropping his 6-year-old daughter off at her mother's. His first assignment from Ed Tobin upon arrival at Warwick HQ was the interview of Katelyn, along with fellow Cocalico PD Sergeant Larry Martin.

Katelyn had gone to the home of a fellow church member to rest after she was done at the crime-scene truck. The two East Cocalico cops swung by in Sweigart's car to request that she accompany them back to police HQ in Warwick for another interview. Katelyn readily agreed. At 2:20 PM, the interview began.

Calmer now, but still distraught, Katelyn told the detective that Kara had met David Ludwig in May and was seeing the older boy three to four times a week at the support group for homeschoolers. The two, who started out harmlessly flirting, quickly developed a strong attraction to each other. She also revealed that about ten times over the last few weeks, her sister had been picked up by David at their house and had gone over to his home to "socialize."

Katelyn told Sweigart that she knew David "well," and considered him a friend. Sergeant Groff produced a copy of Ludwig's Pennsylvania driver's license faxed over to them from Harrisburg, and Sweigart asked Katelyn if this was the young man who'd come to their house and shot her parents. Katelyn said it was. They had their positive ID. The interview ended at 3:30 PM, an hour and ten minutes after it started.

Mr. and Mrs. Ludwig had been brought in for questioning. Detective Zimmerman handled the interviews. Greg Ludwig, an airline pilot, and his wife Jane, a homemaker, were a quiet and devoutly religious couple, and long-time residents of Lititz.

Chief Garipoli reported that Ludwig's parents were cooperating with police "despite their own misery." Warwick's top cop described them as shocked and devastated. "They just don't know. Mom's been in tears a lot and Pop is in total shock."

Greg and Jane Ludwig, however, maintained their composure, being a reserved pair, and readily answered all questions about their son David. During that initial interview, Mr. Ludwig was asked of possible locations his son might have been headed to, and he mentioned a hunting cabin in Juniata County, a couple of hours' drive northwest of Lititz. Once Mr. Ludwig had given him the directions to the cabin, Zimmerman passed it off to the state police and they immediately dispatched a helicopter to check it out and see if David was hiding out there with his believed-to-be-abducted girlfriend.

Although the couple was not accompanied by a lawyer, their pastor, Thomas Gotwalt, never left their side.

Down in Senatobia, Mississippi, 60-year-old Steven Borden, the senior member of the Borden family, and Michael's oldest brother, was out of town shopping in Memphis with his wife Sharon. When they returned home, a panicked message from their nephew Jamie awaited them. Steven fell into a state of shock upon learning the horrible news. He confesses not remembering much about those early hours, which stretched into days. Somehow they managed to make travel arrangements and found themselves flying up to Pennsylvania the next day to help with the grim task of burying his brother and sister-in-law.

Later on Sunday, Kayla Jeffries, a friend of Kara Borden, turned up at the Lititz Borough PD, placed a cell phone on the counter and told Officer Jared Hahn that the phone belonged to Kara Borden. She had gotten it from a friend, Merle Martin, who had found it that morning beside a road that led to the interstate highway. The girl who stood before Hahn said she knew it was Kara's, as she had called Kara's number and Martin had answered. She arranged for Martin to turn over the phone to her.

David Ludwig's discarded cell phone was initially reported to have been turned in separately by Pastor Tom Gotwalt when he accompanied the Ludwigs in their interview with police. Mrs. Ludwig had positively identified it as her son's phone. The phone, in actuality, had been turned over to police by a friend of David's who had found the phone not far from where Kara's was stashed.

The location where the phones were found was helpful in determining the direction in which the fugitives had fled. It suggested the couple were headed for the interstate, and Tobin and Geesey agreed that they should call in the FBI for assistance, given that the two investigators believed David and Kara were fleeing the state. That possibility made it a federal case. There was also the real possibility of a kidnapping, a federal offense.

Case manager Geesey and lead investigator Tobin agreed an Amber Alert should be issued. Amber Alerts (named after Amber Hagerman, a 9-year-old Texas girl abducted, raped and murdered by a known child predator in 1996) are taken very seriously. There are strict criteria for issuing an Amber Alert, as defined by the U.S. Department of Justice; law enforcement is required to use the "best judgment approach based on evidence." The first component that must be met was the hardest for Geesey and Tobin to state unequivocally. That was, that an abduction had occurred. The overriding element, however, of a "risk for seriously bodily harm or death" made the step an easy call for the detectives. The Pennsylvania State Police headquarters in Harrisburg was informed of the decision and they handled the mechanics of issuing the country-wide alert.

Chief Garipoli addressed the media and spoke of the situation:

"We believe that Kara was taken against her will, and until I hear otherwise, Kara is a victim and our main priority is to get her back here with her family."

If they were wrong, and Kara wasn't kidnapped, the authorities had a real-life Romeo-and-Juliet murder case on their hands—forbidden love and murder. Tobin knew what that meant: the media types would be coming out of the woodwork to cover this story, cameras and tape recorders all pointing at him. Ed Tobin hated cameras.

"It's completely insane, completely insane," Lancaster County, Pennsylvania, Coroner Gary Kirchner said on an NBC-TV report. "This isn't a Romeo-and-Juliet deal. This is far worse than that."

Tom Mannon, who lived a couple of doors down from the Bordens, told MSNBC-TV what he knew of the young lovers:

"The boy was infatuated with Kara, that the commonality there was their homeschooling. And there was evidently some kind of bonding that really happened between them. And neither sets of parents wanted that to develop, and so, you know, they said it had come to a point where it has to end, and so they responded by doing it on the sly."

Reba Zimmerman, the Bordens' housekeeper said on CBS-TV that Cathryn Borden ". . . was concerned that Kara was very boy crazy, just like many young teens, but she was e-mailing back and forth with me and she just poured her heart out to me as to 'What should I do?' And 'What a situation,' you know, just trying to avoid tragedy."

Besides the comparison to the star-crossed lovers in Shakespeare's immortal play, there was another story David Ludwig's was being compared to, after his mad dash out of Pennsylvania and into America's Heartland: the story of 19-year-old Charles Starkweather.

Starkweather, unlike Ludwig, was a high school dropout and an out-of-work loser who bore a striking resemblance to then-popular actor James Dean. A former warehouse employer called Starkweather "the dumbest man in the world," having had to fire him for laziness and incompetence. He was, however, smart enough to elude a massive police manhunt for eight weeks.

Starkweather's brief flame of notoriety was sparked on December 1, 1957, in Lincoln, Nebraska, when he murdered a gas station attendant in a robbery.

Frustrated by his meager earnings and his inability to marry his girlfriend, 14-year-old Caril Ann Fugate, he went on a killing and robbing spree. His victims included three members of Fugate's family. Eerily similar to the Borden murders, Starkweather went to Caril Ann's house, argued with and shot her stepfather and mother, and strangled her 2-year-old sister. Caril Ann got home just in time to witness all three murders. Inexplicably, she left with Starkweather, and watched him kill seven more people. The murderous rampage shocked and engrossed the nation much as the Ludwig story would a half-century later. By the time he was caught, on January 29, 1958, in Douglas, Wyoming, eleven people had been left dead in Starkweather's wake.

The embittered loner's flame was finally snuffed out in the Nebraska electric chair on July 25, 1959. Caril Ann Fugate got life in prison, but was paroled in 1976.

Starkweather's story inspired directors like Quentin Tarantino and Oliver Stone to make movies such as *Badlands*, *Wild at Heart*, *True Romance*, *Kalifornia*, and *Natural Born Killers*; all were based on the 1950's most famous serial killer.

The runaway teenage lovers/murderers theme wasn't the only thread that connected the two desperate fugitives. There was also the atmosphere of change that seemed to surround both their times. In the Cold War years of the 1950s, rock and roll, Elvis and James Dean had the adult population unnerved, just as the rise of the popular media and Internet spelled another monumental change for kids of the 21st century. This was the stuff of 24/7 new programs. CNN, FOX, MSNBC and Court TV were all in attendance, microphones and cameras ready.

FOUR

The Morgue

The bodies of Michael and Cathryn Borden were brought to the Lancaster County Morgue located on East King Street in downtown Lancaster. The autopsies were actually conducted in the basement of the Conestoga View nursing home, just one floor above the morgue. The bodies arrived by ambulance early in the evening of Sunday, November 13, and were placed in the refrigeration vault to await the pathologist's scalpel the following Monday morning.

As with all Pennsylvania counties—besides the big cities of Pittsburgh and Philadelphia, which have medical examiners—the coroner is an elective office. There are sixty-six counties; of them six have a physician as a coroner. Lancaster County has a physician/surgeon as a coroner, Dr. Gary Kirchner. In the Commonwealth, funeral directors, nurses and paramedics are all eligible to be coroners.

In the Lancaster County Coroner's Office, besides Dr. Kirchner, there is a top senior deputy, two senior deputies below him, a row of field deputies, a row of emergency room deputies, a forensic pathologist and one administrative assistant. The job of performing the autopsies on the Bordens was left to Forensic Pathologist Dr. Wayne Ross.

"Our mission is easy," said Dr. Kirchner. "We are to determine the nature of a death and causes of a death. The cause is the pathologic reason for somebody to die, and as I am pleased to tell you, if Wayne Ross and I can't tell you how you died, we're in trouble. The nature of death is sometimes extremely easy, sometimes extremely difficult, but I think it's necessary for everybody to understand that that's what the coroner is all about."

Dr. Ross heads a medical/legal investigative team where everything, including the autopsies, is interconnected. The coroner team, in the form of the deputy coroners at the crime scene, examine the bodies and the scene. They then reconstruct what happened and how it happened. As Ross explained, their purpose is three-fold: one, to get the truth out, second, to aid in the crime-scene investigation and third, to help the police and the district attorney in whatever they deem necessary in cultivating the case to fruition.

Michael Borden had been shot in the back of the head. Dr. Ross said it was a "distant gunshot wound," meaning the 9mm bullet had been fired from a distance of "three to four feet or greater." Had the shooter been closer, there would have been powder burns or "stippling" in the area of the wound.

According to Dr. Ross, it was "lights out" for Michael Borden almost immediately, since the bullet severed his brain stem at the base of his skull. Among other things, the brain stem controls the heart rate, respiration and consciousness. The bullet's path continued through the brain and exited from his forehead with the projectile being recovered from the doorframe. The autopsy revealed nothing else that was out of the ordinary. Michael Borden was a healthy 50-year-old Caucasian male.

Cathryn Borden was shot in the right side of the head after the bullet passed through her right hand. Apparently Mrs. Borden knew what was coming and instinctually threw up her hands in a defensive gesture while turning her head away from the shooter. Using vectors, Ross found that the trajectory path was from back to front, right to left and upward. The bullet was removed from the frontal lobe. The vectoring would help determine where the shooter had been standing when he shot Mrs. Borden. But "the bottom line," said Ross, "was, the kid was a good shot."

Ross elaborated: "To shoot both people in the head from some distance in a matter of seconds is very difficult to do. Cops almost always miss in a shootout, and this kid didn't miss twice."

As was the case with her husband, Cathryn Borden was a healthy 50-year-old whose life had been ended by a well-placed bullet to the head.

FIVE

A Private Religious Couple

Michael Borden had grown up in a Catholic home with five siblings in Hannibal, Missouri, the bucolic and whimsical hometown of Mark Twain, the towering 19th-century literary figure. Michael's elder brother Steven remembers it as a great place to live in the 1950s. The sons of a middle management cement factory worker, the three Borden boys and three sisters were comfortably provided for in a time and place when people thought themselves blessed to be that lucky. The Bordens never owned their own home, but the kids marked their lives and categorized their fond memories by the succession of rented homes they dwelled in.

There was also the small farm their grandparents owned in the country, where the Borden brood congregated, that made their respective childhoods so special. Steven waxes nostalgic when recounting the adventures that he and his brothers experienced when they explored the caves that honeycombed the area, and fished on the mighty Mississippi River. It was a childhood worthy of Twain's immortal characters, Tom Sawyer and Huck Finn.

After attending the local Catholic primary schools, and not being from a wealthy family, Michael, the second youngest, put himself through Northeast Missouri State University—now Truman State—in Kirksville and graduated in 1977. He was the first member of his family to earn a college degree. Initially he studied to be an architect, but switched to graphic arts after deciding on a career in printing. After finishing college he joined his brother Steven in Senatobia, Mississippi, to work for the publishing giant RR Donnelly. He married his high school sweetheart Cathy and settled down to raise a family.

Brother Steven professes not to understand why his little brother left the faith of their youth to become a member of a Christian Fundamentalist church, but according to Steven, at least Michael did not try to convert him.

"Mike was always smart and bookish, very serious and industrious, you could say. He never was really what you would call *one of the boys*. He wasn't much into sports and hanging out watching TV and drinking beer. It was not like he wasn't social, because he was, and he liked good company as well as anyone. It was just that he was a little more focused and straight," Steven said.

Cathy, Steven related, was the "sweetest person you could ever meet." She was a devoted wife and mother, and anybody who knew her would be hard-pressed to utter an unkind word about her.

Cathy and Mike quickly brought sons Justin and James into the world with a hiatus of some ten years before Katelyn was born, followed by Kara a year later, and David three years after that.

Mike quickly moved up the ranks at RR Donnelly in the customer service division, but after ten years was wooed away by the plant manager, who took a position at rival Swiss printing conglomerate Ringier AG in North Carolina. While working there, Mike considered going into business himself, partnered with a few colleagues, and building a digital printing plant, but eventually opted to stay under the umbrella of corporate life. Brother Steven says digital printing was *really* new then, and the start-up would have taken a sizeable investment of time and money from Mike.

"He was just not ready to take such a big step," Steven said. "He had job security and a good salary right where he was. Mike had a family to think of."

But apparently Cadmus in Lititz made an attractive enough offer for the Bordens to pull up stakes again and move to the distant and foreign Northeast. For a Southern boy born and bred, and a Fundamental Christian to boot, there must have been some serious hand-wringing in the North Carolina home of the Bordens before the decision to relocate was made. Once it was made, however, Mike Borden forged ahead with a confidence that was typical of him. If he was ever uncomfortable with the change of venue, it never showed to fellow employees or neighbors. Michael Borden, if nothing else, was a man who knew what he wanted out of life, and that was love of family and God.

Catherine Hart had been on the job at Cadmus publishing nine years when Michael Borden was hired away from a rival company in North Carolina in 1995 and brought to Ephrata. Hart was the digital services team leader for the medical and scientific publishing giant, and she studied the man closely, since he would be her immediate boss for the foreseeable future.

Cadmus, part of Cenveo Incorporated, is the third largest graphics communication company in North America, describing itself in company literature as

> ... *a leading provider of print and visual communications, with one-stop services from design through fulfillment. Cenveo's broad portfolio of services and products include commercial printing, envelopes, labels, packaging, publishing and business documents delivered through a network of production, fulfillment and distribution facilities throughout North America.*

Hart knew her company had ardently courted Borden for his services, and had lured him away from the competition with what must have been an attractive salary. She knew his predecessor, the vice president of Science Press Division, had made $120,000 a year as the pre-press director, so for Cadmus to land the 40-year-old experienced executive and move him north, they had to be paying him the princely sum of at least $150,000. That was an awful lot of money for this part of the state.

Borden would be overseeing processing ads, front page makeup, and anything in a digital format: desktop page makeup and any electronic deliverables such as PDF files for online content. The department was responsible for making sure that anything that had to be handed off for printing was correct. Back in 1995 the digital age had not yet fully arrived, so Michael Borden needed to supervise the scanning area where all the film and camera work were done. Cadmus, a $2 billion-a-year company, got the right man to run the department.

Michael Borden stood about 5'10' and weighed over 200 pounds. He was a bit chunky in build, but he would lose over 60 pounds after watching his sister die of cancer. That had scared him into being more careful about his health, he told a co-worker. He didn't lose the weight in a drastic diet, but true to his nature, it was over a methodical two-year period. He explained his successful weight loss by saying he ordered just one burger at McDonald's rather than his usual two. It was an example of his innate frugalness that he had punched new holes in his belts rather than buy new ones.

He appreciated practicality and modesty in others. One year for Christmas Catherine Hart's team gave him a clipboard that was made from recycled circuit boards. He loved it and used it every day.

His most prominent feature was his large head and round face. Blue-gray eyes and a mustache gave him the appearance of a pleasant-looking and non-threatening man. He was soft-spoken with a very subtle Southern accent.

The move to southeastern Pennsylvania to assume his new position did not go smoothly. Borden had to shuttle back and forth to Charlotte for months to see his family until the house was sold. The new job and his itinerant lifestyle did not suit the straight-laced family man, so he was relieved when the old house sold and the family finally settled into a townhouse in Ephrata, until a more spacious home could be found. Within months Michael Borden found an attractive house on Royal Drive in nearby Warwick Township. He and his family moved into their brand-new home in the spring of 1997.

Catherine Hart said Cadmus employees only knew Michael Borden 9 to 5.

"Mr. Borden was very private about his personal life. We knew very little of his life outside the walls of the company," she related, "except that he had a number of children, that his wife didn't work and that she homeschooled the kids. Mr. Borden rarely socialized or took part in company social functions."

His subordinates at work knew he was a religious man, because when he first arrived in Lancaster County, he'd asked different people at work about churches in the area that he and his family could attend. The one that he chose was Monterey Bible Chapel. It is a small Christian Fundamentalist congregation where, according to company gossip, the women sat separate from the men at church services. That was kind of shocking to Catherine Hart. She didn't think that such conservative churches still existed in the area, despite knowing, like most long-time residents, that Lancaster County was very conservative and *very* religious.

Michael would go on to become a church elder and Sunday schoolteacher for the congregation. Michael was "a bit of a perfectionist," one of his fellow elders, Bill Bradford, said. "He wouldn't preach a sermon until every 'i' was dotted and every 't' was crossed."

Borden talked little about his faith, keeping it private, and he never proselytized. There was one time, however, that his underlings got a peek at his beliefs.

A female employee had visited him at his office to give him her notice. As the story was related, Borden asked the woman why she would leave a company where her supervisor was a man who has accepted Jesus Christ as his lord and savior. The woman didn't know what to say; she was flabbergasted by the remark.

Cathryn had the same perfectionist streak, Bradford said. Both were "mighty warriors of prayer": "If you were in Mike Borden's Palm Pilot, you were prayed for."

Hart once saw a side of the man that pleasantly surprised her. Not long after he'd joined the company, Hart brought in her newly born granddaughter and wanted to show her off to her fellow employees. Michael Borden asked Hart if he could hold the infant and he "positively beamed while cradling her in his arms." It was a heartwarming scene from a man who had never let down his guard and never showed a softer side. He, according to Hart, was "normally all business."

Once he told some of his senior subordinates how he wanted them to treat their underlings. They were to be like him and be very strict with them, and make it clear that there were certain expectations of them that they were to fulfill. He then told them a story about how he'd handled a problem employee at his last post.

As he told it, a female subordinate had come to work wearing high heels. He said he realized that she was doing that so she could get out of working jobs that required her to stand for long periods of time. Borden knew she didn't like to perform those particular jobs. He made her go home and change her shoes, because he was not going to let her "dictate what kind of job she was working on."

Although a pleasant, friendly man, he made sure

that all were aware that he was the boss. In one instance he had all the workers take down the *Dilbert* cartoons that they had posted in their cubicles. The daily *Dilbert* strip poked fun at office life and was a daily staple in the funny pages of newspapers across the country. Borden said posting their favorite strips showed "a poor attitude toward management." To Catherine Hart and her colleagues, his stance seemed excessive, but Mr. Borden didn't like dissension.

Borden wanted everyone to do what he wanted, and didn't solicit opinions from his charges. One time he called Hart into his office to tell her who he had selected to be promoted to his old position of site director, when he was elevated to site leader. For the first time ever, he asked Hart for her thoughts on his selection, a man, and like Hart, a valued employee. Surprised at being asked her opinion, Hart felt a frank appraisal on her part was called for. She told her superior that the man in question, whom she had worked with, was a known alcoholic who had a habit of calling in sick on Mondays when everyone knew he was nursing a hangover. The man often left work early and was out of touch for long stretches of time. Hart told her boss he was good at what he did, but in no way would he make a good manager. Michael Borden got red in the face with anger and dismissed Hart from his office.

The very next day, Hart, a senior staff member, was called into the company's Human Resources office and was read a bulleted list of items detailing why she wasn't doing her job as expected. Many of the items seemed to be nit-picking, such as the *Dilbert* cartoons and that her out-going voice mail message was too rigid. She was "knocked for a loop" by the accusations and had no idea that Mr. Borden was "so concerned about her performance."

That same day, Hart later discovered that Mr. Borden had called in a girl who worked for Hart and told her the company was expecting Hart to quit and asked if the girl was interested in assuming Hart's position. Hart never did quit.

Michael's subordinates only got one brief glimpse of his wife Cathryn. It was at a Christmas party early on, and it was the last time she would attend a company function. Michael Borden rarely attended them himself. According to Hart, before Borden's employment at Cadmus, the company had an active social calendar arranged by a company activities committee. After he took over, the committee was left to wither away, with Mr. Borden "making excuses" that there wasn't any money in the budget for it. Consequently the company functions were fewer and fewer, including the annual Christmas party. It used to be a gala event held outside, but under Michael Borden, it became a rather mundane company lunchroom buffet.

When he was in the vicinity, everyone kept quiet and went about their work. There was no hanging around the water cooler. To those who worked under Michael Borden, he was a taskmaster, but he was highly valued by the corporation for his management skills. He also was "great" with clients, said Hart, showing a much more jovial and friendlier side than what fellow Cadmus employees saw.

"He was very well-liked by customers," Hart said,

"since he was very responsive to their needs. It was a very personable and likeable face that he showed to the customer."

Hart said she disagreed a lot with her boss about management philosophy, but one incident stood out in her memory. Back in 1996 she recalls that she was gushing with excitement about getting hooked up to the Internet at home, and was now able to tap into the wealth of information available to her. She was especially thrilled because it would help her in the college course studies that she was taking at the time. Mr. Borden was not impressed. He had told her with an air of authority that, other than "recreational activity, the Internet will never amount to anything."

Hart was "blown away" at the time by her boss's lack of vision, especially since Cadmus was on the cutting edge of the digital revolution.

Early on Monday morning, November 14, 2005, Cadmus team leaders began receiving phone calls from Human Resources. The news was bad: Michael Borden and his wife Cathryn had been murdered. Hart got the call from her team leader while she was getting ready to go to work, and she immediately began calling people who worked under her. Hart said she did not want them hearing the shocking news once they arrived at work.

That Monday, everyone walked around the workplace in a state of shock. Catherine Hart sounded a familiar refrain when such a tragedy happens:

"You hear about stuff like this on TV, but it's always so removed. But to think that it was someone you knew, that you saw every day and interacted with, and that they would not be there when you went to work, was just horrific. For days we were all just numb."

The company brought in some offsite Employee Assistant Program (EAP) people to assist anyone in need of counseling. Hart said she was not aware of anyone seeking out the EAP hirees, because it still was too much of a shock. Typical of the conservative community, friends resorted to consoling one another.

Cadmus offered up no response or official statement on the tragedy, and no company officers were made available for comment to the media. According to a number of employees, the company asked them to follow suit. It was an unusual stance for a large corporate entity to take after losing a senior manager in such a tragic way. It was just another facet of the case that was as curious as it was intriguing.

Tina Shyver-Plank joined the company in 2004, working in composition as a proofreader with some additional experience in administrative work, digital ads, issue management and special projects. She shared Michael Borden's abiding faith in Jesus Christ. Shyver-Plank immediately had taken a liking to the vice president and site manager when she joined the company. She found him unfailingly polite, a fair boss, extremely competent and "spiritual." The 37-year-old Plank found it refreshing after having worked for numerous publishing companies that "stripped your soul" in the workplace.

"Mike was faith-based," Plank said, "with his Christian values not just evident in his personal life, but also in his work life. His caring and compassion for his employees showed. The mutual respect he imbued among associates, the appreciation of the individual, and the caring for the community were cornerstones of Cadmus philosophy under his command at the company. I gained a sense of healing and peace after having worked for soulless giants."

With any downsizing or restructuring dilemmas, according to Shyver-Plank, Mike labored to ensure that as many people as possible retained employment across company locations.

She said Borden "was not fond of having to do what was not his initiative action. He ran the company intelligently and compassionately and engendered great respect. People mattered to him."

Even two years after his untimely death, she still feels the pain of losing her boss in such a horrific way.

"I can tell you that I dearly loved Mike. We all loved him, of course. I would like to see a book do his beloved memory justice. God forgives the assassin, as must we all and surely do, but our hearts are torn asunder and forget we cannot. I *talk* to Mike each day in my own way, for he, in the brief time I knew him, made a positive difference. Mike possessed [a] keen intelligence, true integrity and real compassion. I've never worked for anyone finer than Mike Borden."

SIX

Best Friends

David and Kara met at the after-school sports program that their homeschooling network subscribed to. The homeschooling co-op had hired a qualified sports coach who had worked in a local school system before retiring and making his services available to the legion of co-ops in the county.

As is their tendency, the teens would hang out after the practices, and the homeschoolers hungry for a little social interaction would make the rounds of the congregating young adults. Pretty young girls never seemed in want of attention. David Ludwig was one of the teen boys who made sure of that. The two seemed to hit it off in a friendly, flirtatious way. During the spring of 2005 they could usually be found in each other's company after the day's athletic practices were over, chatting and laughing, indistinguishable from the dozens of other kids around them.

Nobody paid any particular mind to the pair as anything other than just friends until a social get-together was held at the Lititz Recreation Center by the Lititz Christian Church, the Ludwig family's place of worship.

Local bands had been hired to play, and refreshments were offered to the throngs of local kids who showed up at the event that warm spring night. According to friends who knew David and Kara, it was the first time that any of them had noticed anything going on between the two.

Kara had been out in the parking lot involved in a heated exchange with an unidentified boy. David saw what was happening and expressed to the kids within earshot that he was "worried" about Kara. When Kara returned to the rec hall, David took her aside and spoke to her privately for several minutes. It set tongues to wagging among their group of friends and acquaintances.

Christen Frederick, a 23-year-old college student, worked with Ludwig at the local Circuit City.

"He was really a good guy," Frederick said. "He was friendly and joked around. I considered him to be a good Christian. He brought his Bible [to work] and read during breaks."

Frederick said she was aware that David was seeing a 14-year-old and he was keeping it secret because of the age difference.

Tiffany Bomberger, 21, said she'd been friends with David for eight years. They met at activities arranged by the local Christian Homeschool Association. "I was floored. I didn't— I didn't know he could do something like that, because he's a great guy. We had a coed basketball team that they were both on, and soccer team that they were both on. And I knew they were friends. I knew they hung out a lot."

Tiffany's brother Isaiah Bomberger was a friend

and fellow homeschooler of David's. He was surprised at the extent of the sexual nature of David and Kara's relationship. Isaiah was quoted as saying, "They were friends, but I couldn't have said they were boyfriend and girlfriend."

Like all the young lovers' friends, he was stunned by the incident, adding that he couldn't believe "the news about the killings."

Brian Lohr is the father of Sam, David Ludwig's best friend. The 49-year-old Lohr says part of being an adult is being willing to admit you were duped, and he was taken in by his young son's friend.

From a human outlook, David never gave him any idea that the teen had the kind of problems that manifested themselves in the fall of 2005. Lohr provides what he considers a lot of "God-given oversight over his kids." One of the things he has always been adamant about is not letting his children drive with "just anybody." He says that David was one of the few young men he would permit to drive his daughter to and from some youth event.

David by all outward appearances seemed to be a normal teenager. Lohr and the teen often conversed, and with ease, over the eleven years he knew him. A father of five children, Lohr believed it didn't seem out of character for him. He didn't get the feeling it was all show, but that it was in David's nature to be mature and respectful. It wasn't until David reached 16 years of age that his troubles began. Brian Lohr, seeing him as often as he did, quickly picked up on David's "girl problems."

Knowing it was nothing unusual for a teenage boy to experience, "what with the raging hormones and all," it still troubled Sam's father. At about that time, Lohr had had some interaction with David's parents, Greg and Jane. He thought there was some supervision at home that wasn't being provided. Again, it was nothing unusual for a teenager "to run the gap between a dad who is not there and a mom who has a lot on her plate." The Ludwigs also had a daughter with Down syndrome, which complicated their lives and monopolized a lot of the busy couple's attention.

The trouble David was having with girls came to a head, or so Lohr thought, when he took an underaged girl to the family hunting cabin in Juniata County in the spring of 2005. After things had settled down between the Ludwigs and the girl's family, Lohr sat down with David, and remembered asking him, "What was that all about?"

David explained that the girl was having trouble at home and felt threatened, and that he'd just wanted to get her away from all that. Lohr had then asked David if he trusted him, and David responded "Sure." Then Lohr suggested that in the future, he bring any troubled kid to the Lohr home and they would talk about it, and see to it that the youth was taken care of. David assured him he would. Still, Brian Lohr's inner sense told him that there were still some serious issues lurking in the head of this tall good-looking kid.

It was at that time Lohr noticed that David, in the interaction with other kids, was hanging out with Kara Borden. Lohr, of course, knew David's age and he also knew that Kara was four years younger.

In the rumor mill among the teens, Brian Lohr caught wind that something was "wrong" between David and Kara. Lohr, at that point knowing David's family as he did, asked Sam to spend more time with David. The elder Lohr was convinced that David was suicidal. Lohr claims to have learned in his 50-odd years not to be wrong about such things.

Brian Lohr never really got to know Kara Borden. She did, however, show up at the Lohr residence and youth events with her sister Katelyn at all hours of the day and night, but they were never allowed in their home by either him or his wife. The Lohrs told their kids to avoid her because she was "trouble in sneakers."

It was Brian Lohr's discernment, from never seeing Kara with parents or with adults around, that she was a disaster waiting to happen. Lohr says he knows all his kids' friends and parents, but with Kara he knew nothing of her or them. Somewhat pedantically, Lohr said that not meeting a kid's parents tells him something about a kid that he doesn't like.

It was also her way of dressing and wearing makeup that disturbed Lohr. He says he wasn't that far removed from being a young man that he didn't see that the 14-year old Kara dressed provocatively.

"Just because the kid is homeschooled and shows up at a church event doesn't mean everything's okay. They can say they are Christians, but that doesn't mean they are acting like one," Lohr said.

About this time, Sam had broken off his friendship with David, and his father had asked him why that was. Sam had told him David was "sneaking out" and seeing 14-year-old Kara, something he'd warned would threaten their friendship. David had assured his friend that it was over between him and Kara, and Sam accepted his word.

Brian had taken Sam and sister Heidi to a local fair that fateful autumn in '05 and "were hanging" out watching a parade when they were approached by a bunch of kids, Kara and David among them. Sam confronted David about why he was in Kara's company. David gave some lame excuse about them just running into each other. Sam didn't buy it.

As it turned out, both Kara and David had had their parents' permission to attend the fair—but not together. Sam later threatened David that he and another friend would go to the authorities and tell them that he was having a relationship with an underaged girl. Once again David promised he would break it off. From that time on, Brian Lohr related that his son claimed to have assumed David was true to his word.

Lohr wasn't overly concerned with David's seeming fascination with guns, being a hunter himself. He felt that it was normal and he never picked up on an obsession on David's part. David wasn't a "redneck who just wanted to go out and shoot something."

Yet Brian Lohr never knew that David Ludwig kept a registered firearm in his car (as his son told him he did). Had he known this to be true, he would never have let any of his children ride in the Ludwigs' car. Loaded firearms not under lock and key, said Lohr, were accidents waiting to happen.

According to the senior Lohr, David apparently had deliberately presented an "image" to the adult world, and only after you scratched the surface did you learn who David Ludwig really was.

"But there was nothing," Lohr said, "that you could call the police on. There were plenty of people who questioned our church [the Lititz Christian Church] about why we didn't do anything to stop David, and I ask, 'What? What could we have done?' We couldn't tie the young man to a bed! That certainly would have gotten us in the paper. We never saw this terrible thing coming."

David's blogs on the popular teen website Xanga exposed what appears to be his messianic complex. Below he talks about his envisioned "place of worship":

For those of you who have abosolutely no idea what the heck I'm talking about here is the scoop, basically about 3 weeks ago both Sam Lohr and myself (David Ludwig [here he inserted a smiling-face emotion]) felt led to clean up the upstairs of my (the Ludwig's) barn to create a place that we could come to after our Monday night and Friday night youth meetings or at anytime to worship and dilligently seek Gods face. The amazing thing about that is neither Sam or I knew the other was thinking/praying about that till about a week later. Since than a bunch of us have gotten together twice to work on the barn and just amazing things have been accomplished . . . it truely is a miracle!! God has enabled far more to be completed than any of us ever imagined! Glory! So now the need is to finish this project Lord willing before next monday. Anyone is welcome to come once it is finished we only ask that you seek Gods face before you come to see if He wants you to be there. If so, be welcome and come!

And this just before the murders in November:

7 years ago Greg Ludwig [David's father] had a vision that this place would be used for "church." now 7 years later, God is beginning a work that is going to produce greater fruit than we can ever imagine; 30, 40, 50, a hundred fold! Our prayer is that The Barn may be a place of worship, where God is glorified, brothers and sisters in Christ are fed the meat of the Word, Jesus is worshipped, and God's will is advanced in His time. "Ask and you shall recieve, seek and you shall find, knock and it shall be opened to you, for everyone that seeks finds and to him that knocks it shall be opened"

Below, from the July 31 entry. Both Kara Borden's and Kayla Jeffries' user names were in the user list for this page:

Ok everyone, here's the scoop. The barn has been progressing extremely well. Thank you Lord!! and thnx a bunch to all you guys who have been helping! But we do have a lot more to do. . . . laugh So today, if anyone is avalible, the plan is to do a "work evening" on the barn. We're gonna start at 8:00 p.m. and see how much we can get done. What primarilly needs to be done is some decore work as well as a lot of cleaning because we've been making quite the mess while we've been working and a lot of stuff is going to need moving. Heres just a little bit of an idea on what everyone can do if they'd like to come help. . . . anyone is welcome!

Girls, bring any old sheets you have (guys you can too!) We're gonna be hanging them on the walls to make the place look a little nicer. Color doesn't matter. You guys can hang all those up and "decorate"

Guys, we've got to finish getting the plastic up on the walls so the girls can hang the sheets. We also need to finish the wall, move furniture, and build some kind of railling for the top of the stairs.

Also everyone can help with cleaning and moving some boxes and stuff around up there that my mom wants out.

And if anyone has any old furniture we can get a crew to pick those up and put up in. Basically many hands make the task light and since so many of you expressed desire to help we thought tonight would be a good night. Don't worry about rides home we'll take care of that. Anyway I'll see most of you at church. God bless you all!!!

David had a good reputation among the girls in his crowd. He was sweet, gentle, respectful and unerringly polite. He loved talking about movies, music, random trips he took and sports—particularly soccer—and he was like that with everybody, not just the girls he was trying to impress. He eagerly engaged the parents of his friends in conversation, especially on religion.

It was the "barn" that was the real embodiment of his interests: being a leader in his own church, where he would impact people and really make a difference. He talked about it incessantly in the months leading up to

November 2005. Sam Lohr caught the fever too, with David, of course, taking the lead. David felt the adults weren't attentive to the religious needs of their offspring. They had a tendency to be dismissive of the younger congregation and took them for granted. David would be there to see to their spiritual needs and engage them in what one friend called, "just the normal stuff teenage kids go through."

David wanted to help his friends with the parenting issues that all the kids experienced at one time or another: who they hung out with, what they could and couldn't do, how they didn't help out enough at home and curfews.

The "barn" was actually a garage on the Ludwig property that he and Sam were fixing up. David had his heart set on it. It would be their place to go and worship, and do their own thing, branch out in their own direction without adults there to lead them in the direction that they thought was best. David and his small circle of fellow homeschoolers and religious devotees would determine their own way. They had just hung some curtains and put in some couches when, as Kayla Jeffries said, "everything happened," and it all came to an end.

Executive Pastor Kevin Eshleman of the Ephrata Community Church concurred with the Borden neighbors in their assessment of Kara as being a "bubbly, outgoing girl." The pastor added that she regularly attended youth group meetings and got along well with her sister.

"In my mind, that generally indicates that things

are going okay at home," the 43-year-old Eshleman opined.

On November 11, just two days before the murders, Ludwig and a few buddies were hanging out at a local school where a play was being performed. The boys were chatting when David made a comment that would later loom large in his friends' collective memories. David told his friends that he believed he "could kill someone and get away with it, disappear and nobody would find me."

Kayla Jeffries is one of David Ludwig's oldest and dearest friends, and was an invaluable source to investigators assigned to the Bordens' homicide case. Kayla is 5'4" with reddish-blonde hair and pretty blue eyes. She has a cheerful, outgoing personality and is very spontaneous and, she says with an impish smile, she will "do just about anything once." It takes her a while to trust people these days, but everyone knows she's a great listener. Kayla loves meeting new people. She says photography is "my favorite thing" and her dream is to be a photojournalist someday. Kayla, who was 18 years old in 2005, is the second of three children of a church-oriented couple, which is seemingly the norm in Lancaster County.

"I will do anything to help a friend," Kayla told the author. "I'm usually laid-back and just go with the flow. I love children and the innocent things they say. I can tend to be too emotional and overly sensitive. I also tend to read too far into things sometimes . . . Hey, I'm a girl."

Kayla relates that she and David, both lifelong residents of Lancaster County, go back to when they were in the sixth grade together and participating in the homeschooling activities afforded to them by the Lititz Home Educators (LHE) support network they both belonged to.

The two got to bond as friends when both played soccer and bowled on the same teams. There was also basketball, volleyball and the outside classes such as speech that were offered by the network. But it was the "Creation" event that the Lititz Christian Church participated in that started Kayla worshipping at David's church.

Creation was a big Christian music festival in Mount Union, Pennsylvania. The four-day event was like a Christian Woodstock, with several bands, and religious and motivational speakers. The two went together and enjoyed the event immensely.

Joining the church also meant they were both taking the weekly Monday night Bible studies classes. Outside their schooling at home by their mothers, the two were virtually inseparable.

Kayla met Kara Borden through a mutual friend and Kara's older sister Katelyn. Kara became part of their circle of friends. Kara, said Kayla, was mature for her age, despite the four years' difference between the two girls. She says the age difference was never an issue, and that Kara fit right in. She explained that Kara was very outgoing and fun, and didn't act like a 14-year-old.

Kara didn't have to try to fit in, she just did. Kayla elaborated about the friendship the three of them had:

"They were both good friends. They were always there when a friend needed them. They would do everything in their power to help that friend out. David, Kara, and I would always have fun even if we were just going to Burger King. Every Tuesday & Thursday we played soccer together. David and I were in the same graduating class before everything happened so we had senior class activities and meetings together. Kara and I would walk to Turkey Hill [a chain convenience store found throughout rural Pennsylvania] and have so much fun being silly "teenagers." There were so many inside jokes we had that none understood besides us, and that in a way is what brought us closer. Yes, they had their relationship and whatnot, but before everything happened, everyone knew our "group" was the three of us. [Sic]

Kayla wasn't really sure, she says, when Kara and David became romantically involved, but it happened over the course of several months. Nobody really knew, she said, until "everything happened." She would later amend that statement by saying the teen affair was "not really public." That would seem to indicate that she did know all along. Kayla was the pair's best friend, and they were in each other's company constantly in their free time, and she admitted they confided in each other. She must have known Kara's fear of her religious parents finding out about the young lovers, and that they would never accept it and make sure the two never saw each other again. As to David being a womanizer according to press reports, Kayla was adamant that he would never knowingly hurt anybody just for his own gratification.

Kayla was at work that day in November when she heard the horrifying news. It was to become "the worst day of my life." Her cell phone rang constantly that morning at work with her friends calling to commiserate and express their shock. She walked around in a daze, senseless. Her mom showed up at work in short order and told her the police wanted to talk to her, and took her home.

Her mother accompanied Kayla over to the crime-scene truck a block away from Kara's house that morning.

In the "three to four" interviews, although shaken by events and scared, she was their "number one contact" in the initial phase of the investigation, says Detective Ed Tobin. To verify information, says Tobin, "We knew if we went to her, we'd get the right answer." Kayla would continue to be questioned weeks after the young couple's capture in Indiana.

SEVEN

Sam

Samuel Lohr has known David Ludwig, as he says, "since forever."

The two became fast friends through the Lititz Christian Church. Sam, one year older than David, thinks they were about 5 or 6 years of age when they began to pal around after church. It was the beginning of a relationship that would see both of them play to the worst in each other and be penalized for it—one severely.

When Sam started homeschooling in the fourth grade, which was when David did too, they began to see each other a lot at the Lititz Home Educators (LHE) network co-op. Sam's mother bore the brunt of Sam's homeschooling, but through the LHE, Sam and David were able to take classes, such as chemistry and biology, that were taught by LHE members who had an expertise in the subject. David was a good student, Sam relates, and very astute. He wasn't "spectacular or a genius or anything," just a hard-working student who always got good grades.

Along with the courses the LHE offered, a member father volunteered to coach volleyball, basketball and soccer. The boys signed up and became even closer friends.

"David was the sweetest guy, and got along with everybody," Sam said. He would go out on a limb for them—which got him into trouble more than one time. He had an incredible passion to do things for other people, and he was one of the most selfless persons I have ever known. David was always smiling and always laughing."

David was one of those people who was friends with everybody. That was something that impressed the slight and small Sam, who was shy, and consequently did not have a lot of friends.

Sam laughs at the memory of a time when he was actually taller than his friend. That, of course, changed when David turned 17 and shot up past him, eventually reaching the height of 6'2", a full 8 inches taller than Sam.

David was not an exceptional athlete, but he could keep up with everyone on the field. The problem he had was that he had always been skinny, the result of a childhood health problem called patent foramen ovale (PFO), a small hole between the two upper chambers of the heart.

"PFO is a common, benign, congenital condition occurring in one out of four people in which the partition between the upper right and left heart chambers fails to close shortly after birth." PFO also is often a stealth condition. "Most people don't know they have this—it's usually a silent condition," says Dr. Meissner of the Mayo Clinic.

In David's case they were being careful, and he was cautioned about overexerting himself.

Nevertheless, Sam said he "could run forever, but he added, "David was very awkward."

David had a sister, Sarah, two years his junior, whom he doted over. He had a lot of grace and patience with Sarah, who had Down syndrome. Because of her handicap, things had to be explained to her a few times, and she had a tendency to talk a lot.

"Sometimes you just tuned her out," said Sam, "but David always listened—he always had time for Sarah. He would walk her through things three or four times until she got them right. He was really, really good with her."

Jane Ludwig, David's mother, was a great mom, says Sam.

"She was very welcoming, always had a smile on her face, and very kind," Sam recalled. He spent a lot of time at his best friend's home "just hanging out," and was always treated like a member of the family.

David's dad Greg was "a really nice guy," though not as outgoing as his wife. But there was a side of Greg, who was an airline pilot, which most people didn't see. It was the way he raised David "to be defensive at any moment" that revealed a troubling paranoia about the man. Sam says that in his opinion, this kind of rearing is what eventually got David into trouble.

Sam and his Dad, like David and his, were avid hunters. There were plenty of times the four of them would, at the spur of the moment, drop everything and go skeet-shooting with clay pigeons or plinking with their rifles. It was good fun, and Sam and David enjoyed their shoots immensely.

There was one time, however, when Sam joined David and his dad, where Greg had "a lot of guns out" that Sam had never seen before or knew that he had. The gun cache included an M-16 and Mini-14 pistols—military assault firearms. Greg said he had plenty of ammo and they could shoot any weapon as much as they wanted.

Greg was a survivalist and believed you had to be prepared for war on American soil. It was this dooms-day scenario that he impressed on his gun-loving son, who very much looked up to his dad.

Sam admitted he thought "all of this was pretty cool when you are seventeen," especially when he found out about the bunker.

Sam finally saw the bunker in the Ludwigs' base-ment a few months before the murders. Sam had always remembered the closet door in the Ludwig basement, and had wondered what they kept in there. One day David showed him, and he was wowed by its existence.

He only saw the bunker once. It was a small, make-shift hovel built with cinder blocks, plywood and bags of lead shot to keep the roof on. It was basically a room within a room. To enter the actual "bunker," you had to get on your hands and knees and use a crawl space at the base. The structure was basically a glorified and aboveground storm cellar.

There were cots for every member of the family, stores of dried and canned food and gallons of water, basically, everything they would need to survive a brief siege. David told him they'd put guns in there, but never showed him where.

According to Sam Lohr, because of the fears his father possessed, David was also convinced that some kind of invasion could happen at any time. Sam related that the best parallel would be the movie *Red Dawn*, where the Russians invade the United States and are fought by young men in guerrilla-style warfare. David owned the video.

"If anything," Sam said, "I felt sorry that the Ludwigs had felt this kind of dungeon practical. Of course, being a guy, I thought it was cool to say you had a bunker in your basement. But not to this kind of paranoid extent."

There was a brief hiatus in the two boys' friendship where, although still friends, they were not constantly in each other's company during their free time. It was around David's 16th and 17th years. It was not anything anyone did that turned them off, just other interests that had them drifting apart. For Sam it was theater and some private method-acting lessons from a notable drama coach in Lancaster County.

It was apparent to Sam during the friendship lapse that David had begun to take an overly strong interest in girls. It manifested itself first with a girl in Hawaii.

The girl (name withheld because of her age) had lived in Lancaster County and David met her through their mutual homeschooling network. Because David's father Greg was a commercial pilot, the family often vacationed in Hawaii. The two teens liked each other, so David made a point of hooking up with her while there. One evening he wound up in her room and in her bed.

Her suspicious father knocked on the door and David leaped out of bed and climbed out the window onto the balcony. The father spotted him. David got into plenty of trouble over that stunt.

Lea was the next paramour of David's to get him

into trouble yet again. Lea was the one who'd run away from home to be with David at his family's hunting cabin in Juniata County. Sam had known that David liked the girl, whom he didn't know, but not to what extent, until the two were found that weekend by a visiting resident of a nearby cabin.

When David started hanging out with Kara, Sam thought this would only mean more trouble for David. David kept his interest in Kara quiet and never even told his best friend.

"She had that look that said, 'I could tease you to death,' and the more I got to know her, the more I was sure that she was a little [expletive]—and she was sneaky about it too," Sam said.

Sam told his friend, whom he was palling around with again, what he thought of Kara, and warned him that she could be trouble. But David said Sam was wrong, and that she was a "sweet, innocent girl." Sam would have laughed in his face if it weren't so serious a problem, considering David's recent experiences with underaged girls. Sam believed David to be "mixed-up."

"When I say David was mixed-up," Sam explained, "I believe it was a combination of wanting the feeling of sex and that connection with someone, but knowing that it was wrong at the same time. Kara had enormous pull on his emotions though, and David was driven by them."

At first Sam wasn't aware that his childhood friend was sexually involved with Kara. He had to know that he was going to her house, but admits he was too naïve to realize that the pair were caught up in a torrid affair—or that "they were actually doing something in there." Although a year younger, David was years ahead in sexual maturity and activity than Sam.

"It was a shock for me when I found out," Sam related. "I remember telling him, 'Man, I can't believe you are actually doing this [sexual relations] with her'. But at the time, I was in a pretty mixed-up state myself, since I had just come off an ordeal that I was actually involved in."

The "ordeal" that Sam Lohr was involved in made David's tryst with the 14-year-old Kara pale in comparison. Ultimately Sam's unfortunate experience led to legal action and an untimely death.

Sam had been a victim as a minor in a sexual molestation case involving his drama coach. Sam had been working for an acting troupe called Maranatha Productions in Lancaster that was run by Dan Neidermyer. Neidermyer was a graduate of Philadelphia College of Bible and did graduate work in radio-TV-film at Temple University. He lived in Lancaster with his wife. Besides being an acting coach, Neidermyer was the producer/director for Maranatha Productions, Inc., a non-profit educational theatre, staging productions throughout the U.S., United Kingdom, West Indies and Scandinavia.

Sam worked with the troupe's mentor for over a year. Neidermyer taught the "method" style of acting made popular by such Hollywood icons as James Dean and Marlon Brando in the 1950s. The acting coach taught it in a way that "opened your emotions up," and challenged Sam "morally." Sam related that there were "very sexual things that I had to run away from." Sam would go to the police with his story.

Dan Neidermyer was charged by Detective Al Leed of the Manheim Township Police Department, Lancaster County, with sexual abuse involving two young boys, one of whom was Sam Lohr.

"He was groping them," said Detective Joe Geesey, "having them perform in the nude while he watched, all in the name of theatrical performing. He was also involved in other things with the other boys, but all he was charged with in regard to Sam Lohr and the other boy was the groping and performing nude situation. The other boys involved would not come forward and be victims."

Neidermyer did all the teaching in the basement of his house. Nobody but he and his student were allowed down there when a lesson was being given. All the lights were turned off and the student would be wearing a blindfold. Sam Lohr didn't need to elaborate.

Neidermyer faced a preliminary hearing that was held on January 9, 2007, and he pleaded "No Contest" to two counts of corruption of minors. He got 5 years' probation and was fined $500. Sam's accusations about the "acting lesson activities" were the first that Neidermyer's wife had heard of them.

Neidermyer was forbidden to leave the state under terms of his probation, and had to register as a sex offender. Those onerous legal stipulations proved to be devastating, since his acting company traveled widely, and performed nationally and internationally. The restrictions, loss of income and the shame caused the acting professional to slip into depression. The 60-year old Neidermyer shot himself at a scenic overlook in Martic Township on March 17, 2007.

Coming off that ordeal, Lohr says he was in an

"unsteady place himself" when he found out David Ludwig was seeing 14-year-old Kara Borden.

"On one hand, I'm saying to myself, 'This is wrong', and on the other, maybe it was okay and something good would come of it," he said.

On the morning of November 13, Sam was getting ready to go to church when his parents called him into their bedroom to talk. He picked up on the fact that both were very quiet and somber. His sister Heidi was acting strangely too. Sam remembers asking them "What's going on, what don't I know?"

His parents gave it to him straight and simply said, "David shot Kara's parents."

Sam was "floored" by the revelation, and couldn't even talk. He had no idea what to think. It was such a shock for him that he remembers little of that morning. Sam knows he ended up at church, but doesn't recall how he got there. He spent the rest of the day in tears, "just bawling," he related.

The 17-year-old remembers thinking, as the shock began to wear off, that he, more than anyone, knew about David Ludwig and his relationship with Kara Borden. He knew he had to talk to someone. He told himself that if they didn't know where the young couple was, maybe there was something he could tell them that might help in the apprehension of his best friend. Sam went to the police.

Sam says he gave them the "whole truth"—which wound up getting him in trouble with the law as well.

Lohr says 90 percent of what was reported about his involvement in the newspapers wasn't true or was grossly exaggerated. As a result, Sam got the cold shoulder by people who knew about his involvement in the case. He was David's friend, and even though the public didn't know him, he became "a bad guy," said Lohr.

EIGHT

Indiana

"It didn't take genius looking at a map to figure he may
be passing through," said First Sergeant Jeff Hearon,
District Investigative Commander of the Indiana State
Police (ISP), District 53. The "he," of course, was a reference to fugitive David Ludwig and his allegedly
kidnapped victim, Kara Borden. A nationwide Amber
Alert had been issued, and descriptions of the fugitives
and the vehicle they were driving were known to every
police department in the country. Sergeant Hearon had
been warned by the Pennsylvania authorities that they
had it on good information that Ludwig might try to
drive west somewhere and "disappear." His trooper barracks were in Putnamville, Indiana, 48 miles west of
Indianapolis, just off Interstate 70 which bisected the
state and was the main route of passage for those traveling east to west. In Pennsylvania, just south of Pittsburgh, I-70 became I-76 and passed through Lancaster.

Dave Cox, 38, a fifteen-year veteran of the state police
and a ten-year member of the SWAT team, is a farm
boy who'd grown up not far from where he worked. On
November 15, 2005, he was a senior officer specializ-

ing in truck enforcement as a road trooper. Another ISP trooper on duty that day was Dave Furnas, a son of a former Indiana state policeman and an eighteen-year veteran trooper. Both men were assigned to cover Hendricks County and because of seniority were assigned day duty.

Master Trooper Furnas was on his usual patrol route along I-70, ten miles west of Indianapolis, on the warm sunny November day when he heard his radio snap to life. It was dispatch with another alert to be on the lookout for a red VW Jetta with Pennsylvania plates that may be heading west on I-70. The dispatcher rattled off the Pennsylvania plate number and informed the trooper there was an Amber Alert for the female occupant.

Observing traffic and keeping a sharp eye out for red Jettas, Trooper Furnas noticed he was getting low on fuel. He got a radio call from fellow Master Trooper Cox, who was a few miles farther west on I-70. Telling Cox he needed fuel, Cox said he would join him at the gas station and they could take a brief break together.

Driving east, Furnas saw a stranded motorist on the westbound side of the interstate at about the 62 mile marker from the Illinois state line. It was a minivan driven by a female. Furnas made a U-turn to check on her. The woman told the officer that she had some help that was on the way. By that time Trooper Cox had caught up to his friend and colleague, and pulled up on the median to check if everything was all right. By hand signals, Furnas indicated that all was well. Cox sped off.

Seconds later Furnas pulled out, crossed the median and continued heading east toward the gas station on Exit 66. At that point Cox, by Furnas' calculations, would have been about a mile in front of him.

Traveling east, Cox figured Furnas would catch up to him before he reached the exit for the gas station. About a mile-and-a-half up the road he saw a red VW traveling west. As the car shot by him, Cox could see the driver turn his head to look at him from across the median as he sped by. The trooper could see it was a white male. He also was pretty sure the car had Pennsylvania license plates. Cox thought he had a good possible sighting of a wanted fugitive.

Cox "called it out" to Furnas over the radio, telling him, "There's one getting ready to come by you that we need to check out."

Furnas made an immediate U-turn, and jumped the median again. He spied Cox's patrol car out of the corner of his right eye, already in pursuit of the suspect car. Furnas "hit the grass again" and bumped up onto the west-bound lane and burned some rubber as the red Jetta lived up to its name and shot by him.

Furnas took the lead in the chase of the Jetta. He was quickly on the tail of the red sedan. He could see there were two occupants, a male and a female, and the plates were Pennsylvania tags. By this time Cox had caught up and followed closely behind Furnas. The two men discussed strategy over the radio and decided to make a felony stop at the Exit 59 ramp that led up to State Road #39. A felony stop is when the patrol car stops a vehicle and the officers don't physically approach the vehicle, but order the occupants out, then position themselves so that the armed officer can take control of the situation.

Dave Cox had been a cop long enough to know this fugitive wouldn't just pull over on their command. He knew there would be a pursuit, as the suspect was wanted for double homicide and possible kidnapping. The suspect, David Ludwig, was a desperate young man, and something dramatic was in the cards for all of them.

At first Trooper Cox did not see the female passenger, but her head finally popped into view, and she then constantly turned to watch the two chase vehicles.

Like his fellow trooper, Dave Cox knew this road well, having grown up in the area and patrolled these very roads for the last fifteen years. He estimated that the pursued Jetta at times reached 100 mph. This could get ugly, he thought.

Furnas steered into the passing lane, sped up and pulled alongside of the Jetta. Cox came right up behind it. The Jetta was boxed in. Furnas made eye contact with the driver to make sure the occupants matched the wanted kids. It was definitely them. Approaching the exit Furnas and Cox made their move, trying to nudge the vehicle off onto the ramp. Furnas said "that's when the car took off."

Furnas went with him and tried to force him over to the shoulder. It didn't work. The Jetta sped ahead and Furnas fell in behind it. Cox followed closely behind his fellow officer. At the top of the ramp, the Jetta turned right, heading north on State Road #39, a two-lane country road with an occasional farmhouse and barn along the way. Motorists didn't encounter a traffic light or stop sign until the town of Belleville five miles up the road.

The Jetta unexpectedly switched over to the left lane and headed straight for a semi–tractor trailer that was headed south. On this rare flat stretch of the road, the trucker stomped on his brakes and tried to get as far over to his right as possible. Furnas could see the smoke bellowing from the tires. With squealing brakes the big 18-wheeler just managed to avoid an ugly head-on with the Jetta, which would have certainly been demolished.

It was apparent to Furnas that the fleeing suspect was trying to force the truck to jackknife and block the road, and afford an escape for himself. Or the suspect might have been trying to get the vehicle to crash, forcing the troopers to stop to give aid to the victims. It didn't work.

Seconds later, he tried it again. This time it was a pickup. Again, he failed. About a mile down the road, Furnas gave "a little tap" to David's rear bumper to "rattle him." At speeds in excess of 90 mph, it can be unnerving, to say the least, but, said Furnas, "It didn't even faze the driver of the Jetta. As a matter of fact, he accelerated and went even faster."

Furnas was glad Cox was behind him and handling the radio, which left Furnas to just drive and focus on the chase.

At the Deer Creek Golf Club on #39, cars have to climb a long rising hill, which Furnas called "a bad one," since both north- and south-traveling vehicles can't see what is over the hump. The Jetta swung into the left lane, blocking any south-bound motorist and leaving himself open to a head-on. Furnas swung in behind him, the both of them passing slower-moving traffic in the right lane. Fortunately for both, there was no south-bound traffic coming over the hill. It was a risky gamble by both pursued and pursuer.

There was more trouble up ahead. Furnas backed

off, knowing a dangerous curve was coming up. The Jetta moved into the left lane as he approached the curve. Just then another semi was barreling south on #39. Hitting his brakes hard, the trucker locked up all his tires, spewing black smoke in the process. At the last second the trucker swerved out of the way, almost sending his back end into a fishtail spin-out. Furnas said the trucker "almost lost it."

Coming up, a steep climb approached as #39 led into the town of Belleville. Furnas once again tapped Ludwig's bumper "just to get his attention." The Jetta moved over to the center-left lane and just missed another south-traveling motorist.

In Belleville, Furnas knew there was a sharp-left turn just before the town center. The Jetta, on the curve, ran a motorcyclist off the road and clipped a U.S. Mail carrier's vehicle stopped for a delivery. Furnas backed off because they were coming up on a traffic light at US #40, which crossed #39. Some northbound traffic on #39 had just gone through the intersection, tripping the light green. Had they not, the Jetta would have had a red light. "Who knows what would have happened had there been crossing traffic with a green light?" Furnas speculated.

Furnas slowed again because of the "pretty good jack" the raised intersection gave a car traveling fast through it. The Jetta, unaware of the bump, went airborne and slammed to the blacktop, hard, but kept to the road.

Right after the intersection, the road took a 90-degree turn to the left. Straightaway was a cul-de-sac. Because of its speed, the momentum carried it on to the dead-end road. Furnas knew the chase was about over.

Seeing his opportunity, Furnas bumped the Jetta hard at about 45 mph to rattle the driver, who was losing control of his vehicle. Furnas forced the Jetta off the road and sent it straight for the solitary tree near the end of the cul-de-sac. The fugitive slammed on his brakes hard. Furnas could see the driver's head lean left as he tried to turn away from the upcoming crash, but Furnas kept the Jetta on course for the tree. At the last second, Trooper Furnas spun his wheel a hard left so he wouldn't take any of the impact of hitting the tree, something the Jetta could now not avoid. Furnas harmlessly hit a wire fence and stopped. The Jetta hit the tree "dead-on" at about 40 mph. Both airbags exploded in the faces of the two Pennsylvania teenagers.

Furnas jumped out and ran to the Jetta's driver's side. Cox, who was seconds behind, got out of his car and approached from the rear. Both men had their 9mm Glock 17s drawn.

Approaching the Jetta, Cox was thinking they had a hostage situation, being that an Amber Alert had been issued by the Pennsylvania State Police. Aiming his gun at the figure in the driver's seat, he gauged he had a clear shot and could take out the fugitive behind the wheel if he pulled a gun on them.

Standing next to the driver's door, Cox could see the suspect was not armed, so in one quick motion, he jerked open the door. When he saw that the driver was strapped in, he quickly unsnapped the seat belt, pulled the driver out of the car and threw him to the ground. Cox jumped on top of him and snapped the handcuffs on him in one practiced and often-used motion.

The kid was apparently dazed by the crash, and the deployment of the airbags—"a wonderful thing," said

Furnas—prevented him from reaching down and grabbing one of the two pistols that had slid onto the front floorboards from under the driver's seat.

At that moment the female passenger emerged from the crashed car, ran around the back and started screaming hysterically at the two troopers. "Don't hurt him, please don't hurt him!"

Furnas didn't know if she was an accomplice or not, saying, "She didn't act like much of a victim at that point." Less circumspect, Cox remembers thinking, "Hostage, my ass. She's a suspect!"

Still pinning Ludwig to the ground, Cox hollered at Furnas, "Put a gun on her!" It took a moment for it to register with Furnas, so Cox felt obliged to holler it again with a little more emphasis on the word "gun." Furnas caught his drift, and put a bead on Kara with his service pistol. The young blonde-haired girl appeared to be just a kid to Cox, the father of two youngsters himself. She continued to scream "Don't hurt him!" in a shrill voice, over and over until Cox hollered back that if she didn't shut her mouth he'd "punch her right in the jaw." The female quit screaming and began to whimper.

It took several moments for her to follow their orders to lie on the ground. When she did, Furnas quickly handcuffed her.

"It really turned my stomach," Cox said, "knowing this guy had killed her parents, and here she was defending him. I didn't have much sympathy for her at that time."

Getting off the fugitive, Cox went over to the car and looked inside. He could clearly see the two handguns that had slid forward from under the seat on the crash impact, and come to rest on the floorboards under the foot pedals. He once again thanked God for the airbags that had prevented Ludwig from reaching for them.

A sheriff's deputy who lived nearby and had heard the crash arrived on the scene to assist the two ISP troopers. Within minutes, several ISP squad cars were on the scene including Sergeant Jeff Hearon's.

After finally calming down, the handcuffed girl asked Furnas if they had been in the news. Furnas, while eyeing the circling helicopters, said facetiously, "Ya think?" With plaintive eyes she then asked if her parents were dead. Furnas lied and said he didn't know, as she had to be properly notified.

NINE

Interrogation

When the pursuit started, Sergeant Hearon was at his post 17 miles away. But when it was announced over the radio that this was an Amber Alert situation, he checked with dispatch, then, along with another officer, got into to his car and sped off to join the chase. He arrived some ten minutes after the crash. Hearon approached the kneeling and handcuffed Ludwig while a helicopter hovered overhead. Hearon, senior officer on the scene, knelt down and placed his hand on the shoulder of the young man and asked him his name. He could feel the suspect shaking, no doubt, Hearon believed, because of the adrenaline rush from the chase and crash. Ludwig said his name and was helped to his feet. Hearon could not retrieve Ludwig's coat from the VW, since he didn't want to disturb possible evidence, so he put him in the back seat of his squad car and turned up the heat to warm the vehicle.

Hearon did a quick inspection of the VW and saw two pistols lying in plain view on the front seat floorboards of the vehicle. He ordered that nobody go into the car, and to get it loaded on a wrecker to be brought back to the post. He then requested over one of the troopers' radios that a detective be sent from the post to take charge of the crash scene. A call from Lancaster was routed to Hearon's cell phone number. Detective Ed Tobin gave him the rundown on what had happened there. Hearon, gauging Ludwig's demeanor, said that Ludwig might want to speak to him. Should the Indiana State Police try to get an interview with an agreeable Ludwig? Tobin unhesitatingly gave him the go-ahead.

After getting behind the wheel of his vehicle, Hearon turned around and spoke calmly to the hand-cuffed Ludwig.

He patiently explained that he understood it had been a long day for him, but he had to ask him some questions. He then read him his Miranda rights and added that he was sure Ludwig had been thinking about what he was going to say and how "It must been weighing on ya." Ludwig finally spoke, saying, "I have a question." He hesitated for a moment and continued, "Are they dead?"

Hearon replied, "What makes you say that?"

"Because I shot them and I think I might have killed them."

The veteran cop told Ludwig that he'd have to back up and tell him the whole story.

In an emotionless voice, David Ludwig then explained, briefly, what had brought him and Kara to this place in the middle of Indiana farm country. Hearon described Ludwig as very calm, and showing "a complete lack of concern or remorse."

On Sergeant Hearon's instructions, Kara Borden

was taken to the trooper post separately by Sergeant Patricia Warczynski.

Back at the Putnamville trooper post, Ludwig was brought into the interview room. Sergeant Hearon read him his rights again and Detective Brian Smith took a seat across from Ludwig.

Detective Hearon: The time now is three past two PM, I'm Detective First Sergeant Jeffrey C. Hearon with the Indiana State Police, PE number [Permanent Employee number—it is like a badge number] five-two-zero-one. Officer present, Detective Brian Smith, PE number five-four-zero-one, and we are speaking to David Ludwig. Am I pronouncing that correctly?

Ludwig: Yes.

Hearon: All right, David, I read you your rights, and you signed a waiver and agreed to speak to us. Is that right?

Ludwig: Yes.

Hearon: Okay, all right, let's go back to what occurred between you and Kara. If you could.

On Saturday night, Ludwig related, Kara had slipped out of her house late, after everybody had gone to sleep, and sneaked into his house, where they'd had sex in his bedroom. Trying to get back into her house at 5:30 AM through a downstairs window, she was caught by her mother, who had been asleep on the living room couch.

As agreed on, after giving her time to get home, he would text-message her to see that she'd gotten back safely. She would then text him back. When he got no reply, he sent three or four more messages. No response. Worried, he called her. She did not answer, so he tried texting her again. After a few minutes, she called him. David could not pick up the phone and talk because he was upstairs and his parents were still asleep. He'd had to go downstairs to call her back.

Kara answered and blurted out to David that she had been caught, and her parents were with her now. David thought she was joking, and told her, "That's pretty funny, what are you really doing?"

After a few seconds of silence at the other end of the line, he realized that she was not kidding. David asked her what they should do now. Kara said he had to come over. He told her that he couldn't do that. He heard more yelling in the background. He then heard Kara yelling at her parents, then she abruptly hung up. He called back a few minutes later and asked Kara again what they should do. David then offered to come over and rescue her from her parents, or he could stay home and get her later, or they could talk this thing out and figure out what to do. Kara was not sure what to do, but told him that he'd better come over immediately, or her parents would start calling people. David told her he was coming to get her, and that he would be armed. Kara asked what if her father was resistant. David gave her a couple of scenarios: either he could get her away in a non-violent way by talking to them, or he could knock them out or "something like that. Or," he continued, "I could shoot them." Kara was unresponsive. After several seconds of silence, she said, "I don't know."

David was asked by Sergeant Hearon if, prior to this, they had ever discussed using violence to get Kara away from her parents. They had, "but not like they ever planned it or anything." They had agreed that "nothing" would ever prevent them from seeing each other again. David told the two cops that he'd never planned any "injuries" against Kara's parents, but he would "be prepared with weapons."

Next to David's room in the Ludwig household was the "hobby room" where the firearms were kept, all fifty-two of them. David picked out four: a Glock 27, a Colt .45, a Ruger .22—all pistols—and a Ruger Mini-14 rifle.

David dressed all in black. Detective Smith asked him about the choice of clothes.

Ludwig: I dressed in black because black is a neutral color, good for camouflage. Also, if someone were to see me, then when I were to re-dress [in different clothes] at a later date, it would be harder to tell because when you have a person in black you are just a person in black—it's harder to describe a person in black.

Hearon asked if he'd worn a mask, and David said no, but he did wear a hat the entire time.

Hearon wanted to know if Michael and Cathryn Borden had known David. He answered that they did, having met him two or three times. Departing from the timeline of the crime, Sergeant Hearon asked how long David had known Kara. David told the two investigators that he and Kara had met back in June, but really didn't get to know each other until homeschool graduation. They'd become close in September.

On the day of the murders, David had taken his father's red VW Jetta and driven to Kara's house, less than three miles away. He'd parked it down the street from 15 Royal Drive. Before getting out of the car, he'd wrapped his Ruger pistol and a buck knife in a blanket and gone to the rear door of the Borden house. David believed Kara's father owned a pistol. He'd knocked on the door and waited, adjusting the blanket so Mr. Borden could see David's weapons when he opened the door.

Mr. Borden saw what David was carrying and told him to leave the guns on the porch. David had concealed his Glock semiautomatic pistol in a belly holster tucked in his waistband under a loose-fitting shirt. Upon entering the house, he was shown to the living room, where Mrs. Borden was seated in a recliner, and he took a seat on the couch. Mr. Borden sat next to him.

According to David, they spoke for the next thirty to forty-five minutes about his relationship with Kara. David said the conversation was not confrontational or emotional "in any way, shape or form." A couple of times their tones got elevated when something he said angered them, but nothing more than that. David suggested the detectives talk to Kara about her parents' demeanor before he'd come over, saying they were calm when he arrived.

Finally Mr. Borden told David that he should go home and tell his parents about his relationship with

Kara and what had transpired there today. Mr. Borden also told David "obviously this cannot continue," and then went on to discuss the "spiritual aspects" of their sinful relationship. Mr. Borden then asked him how he thought they should resolve this. David told him that he had no idea. Kara's father went on to say that "this had to end," explaining that Kara was not ready for this relationship—or any kind of relationship. David asked if he could ever see Kara again, but got no response from her dad. Mr. Borden concluded the conversation by repeating that David should talk to his parents and come back to him at a later date. With that, Mr. Borden told him there was nothing more to say and that it was time for David to leave.

Mr. Borden got up from the couch and David followed him. As Mr. Borden reached down for the doorknob, David saw his opportunity. He drew the Glock from under his shirt and shot Michael Borden once in the back of the head. Michael Borden was dead before he hit the floor. David told the two Indiana State Police officers that he was not aiming, so he didn't know where he'd hit him, but that he was a "good shot."

David said he didn't know if this meant anything, but he "did not mean to kill them." He claimed not to know whether or not they were okay. He had thought about knocking him out instead, but Mr. Borden was a lot bigger, and he was not very confident of his fighting skills, saying he was afraid of getting into a fistfight with the older man. Those fears made him shoot Mr. Borden.

David then turned toward his left and saw Mrs. Borden getting up from the recliner in the living room. She covered her face with her hands as the pistol-wielding Ludwig turned to her. David assumed a combat shooting stance and pulled the trigger. Cathryn Lee Borden fell back without a sound.

Ludwig and Detective Smith had this chilling exchange on the shooting of Mrs. Borden:

Ludwig: Dad is down. I turned to walk down the hallway, turned around to my left and saw Mom getting out of the recliner. I shot again and did not aim. I'm not sure where the bullet entered. She was turned slightly to the side of me. At which point I shot her.

Smith: Okay, Dave, as you go down the hallway here [pointing to the location on Ludwig's drawing of the crime scene] after you shot the father, you say Mom is trying to get out of the recliner seat, you shot her. Did you see where you hit her?

Ludwig: No, I didn't. I don't remember if I got a good grip on the gun or not. I'm not sure if I used two hands or one hand.

Smith: Did she react as if she had been shot?

Ludwig: She slumped back down in the chair, rising to falling.

Hearon: Did she say anything to you?

Ludwig: No. Neither of them did. I didn't hear a thing anyway because my ears were ringing. I couldn't hear for an hour to two hours easy after the reports of the pistol.

Smith: Why did you feel you had to shoot Mom? What was going through your mind at the time?

Ludwig: Panic, I guess. Really have no idea. I had not thought about— Kara and I talked about it later—and I had come to a decision . . . it would have been a much wiser decision to just to have shot her dad—if I had to shoot anyone. Preferably, not shoot anyone. But if I just shot her dad, I coulda gotten away from her mom. Just reaction, I honestly don't know what was going through my head.

Smith: Okay.

Ludwig: There were no feelings of vengeance. I had no desires to hurt her, just reaction.

Turning his attention to the kitchen on his right, he saw that Kara and Katelyn were no longer there. They had been listening and watching the confrontation. When the gunfire erupted, they had run to the back of the house. David hurried into the kitchen, then went down a short hallway to the dining room. No one was there. He proceeded up the stairs to the second floor. David knew that Kara's siblings' rooms were to his left. He told Hearon and Bridges that he'd had no desire to do them any harm, so he went straight to Kara's room on the right. She was not there. His heart pumping hard from the adrenaline rush, he ran downstairs and out the back door.

As he scanned the backyard for Kara, he heard a popping sound from above. He turned around and looked up to see Kara's younger brother David kick out the window screen and attempt to climb out the window onto the roof so as to make his escape. David had his gun concealed, but yelled up to David that he wasn't going to hurt him and that he should go to the neighbors. David began yelling for Kara. Ludwig circled around back, searching the adjacent yards before retracing his route back out front. Once he reached the road, David said, he started jogging to the end of a cul-de-sac, through a wooded area, before returning to his car after a few minutes. He drove down Royal and turned left on Rudy Dam Road and then headed for his home, not sure what he would do next. Before he got to Owl Hill Road, he had second thoughts. He decided to look for Kara again. He slowed and turned his car around. Just then he saw Kara running down the street toward him. Pulling over, Kara quickly jumped into the front seat.

In her excitement, Kara said she was "so thankful to see you." Kara explained that she got scared when she was looking for him and couldn't find him.

David drove through Lititz, taking back roads wherever he could. Before getting on I-222, David pitched both his and Kara's cell phones out of the car. He explained when asked by Sergeant Hearon that he was afraid they could be traced by the imbedded GPSs.

David asked Kara if she knew that he had shot her parents. She said she did. He then asked her if she wanted to come with him. Once again she said she did.

They had $67 between them, the clothes on their backs and the weapons.

On the interstate, stopping to get gas, they found an automated teller machine and withdrew $300 from David's account.

Detective Smith asked about the gun David had used. He told Smith he'd used the Glock with hollow-point bullets (hollow-points fragment upon striking an object, causing maximum damage to the target). Smith asked him where the Glock was now. David replied that it was under the front seat of his car.

"How far were you from the father when you shot him?" asked Smith. David replied "from here to the end of the table." Asked to clarify, David said had been seven or eight feet away when he shot Mr. Borden. Queried about how many shots he'd fired, he replied "Just one time for Dad and one time for Mom." David claimed he did not know where the victims were struck by the .40-caliber slugs, but thought it was in the torso area. David demonstrated how he'd shot and posed in a Weaver stance—a police combat stance with fist cupped at the gun butt while in a squatting position.

David said that before Mr. Borden hit the floor, David was turning in Mrs. Borden's direction. According to David she was halfway out of her seat when he shot her. David drew a schematic of where everybody had been in the house at the time of the shootings.

Out of the corner of his eye he saw a flash of movement in the kitchen area. He wasn't sure if it was Kara or Katelyn. That was why, he said, he'd gone off in that direction calling Kara's name.

Sergeant Hearon's intuition told him that David was cutting Kara's ties. He had shot both Bordens because he didn't want anybody left for her to run home to.

Hearon asked what their intentions had been when they drove away from Lititz:

Smith: Where were you guys headed? What did you have planned?

Ludwig: We had no destination. Didn't know. Our goal was to get as far west as possible. We had no money beyond like three hundred dollars that I drew from my account . . . filled up the car with gas twice, bought some clothes and personal care stuff, which is in the trunk of the car. I was hoping to sell the car somehow, get a cheaper car, a better car that the cops wouldn't be looking for.

Smith: Okay.

Ludwig: I also had a platinum ring I was hoping to sell, and a gold necklace. Beyond that, I was just hoping to get a job, get married and start a life.

Detective Smith said it appeared that they'd had a "pretty intense relationship with the sex and everything." He asked if Kara was pregnant. David said no, not that he was aware of, but they'd thought she was last month, and that's when they'd started to plan an escape.

Smith asked about their most recent plans to run away.

David said it was going to have been next weekend while the Bordens were attending a wedding. He explained that they weren't going to take his dad's car, but another they could pack with their things. He also said he had some investments he planned to liquidate.

Back in Lancaster, DA Don Totaro was at the Warwick Township police station when the pursuit appeared on TV. He was surprised to find this story on national television, and was relieved when Ludwig was finally taken into custody. Ed Tobin was on the phone in his Warwick PD office with the Indiana authorities while the chase/apprehension was being broadcast. Joe Geesey had missed it—he caught it later on videotape—but the news of it prompted him to start making arrangements to get out to Indiana to interview Ludwig and bring him back to Lancaster.

Geesey had mentioned to Special FBI Agent Rick Etzler, who was in charge of the Harrisburg office, that he had to make arrangements to get out to Indiana. Etzler told him to hold off until he checked on something. He returned with some good news. The U.S. Department of Justice's jet, which was used almost exclusively by the U.S. Attorney General and the Director of the FBI, had become available after a charter had been canceled. Etzler pulled a few strings and managed to charter the jet for the Lancaster contingent. The Feds' jet could pick them up in Lancaster and fly them to Indianapolis that day. Geesey was thrilled. Lead investigator Ed Tobin was not—he hated to fly.

Joe Geesey, Ed Tobin, FBI Agent Jeff Blaney (the FBI liaison for transport of investigators to Indiana) and Detective Kerry Sweigart boarded the jet at around 4:30 PM for the hour flight to Indianapolis.

TEN

A Difficult Victim

Once back at the post with Kara, Sergeant Warczynski turned her over to Detective Sergeant Deny Bridges. Other than being a veteran investigator for the Indiana State Police, the 48-year-old Bridges was a curious choice for baby-sitting the petite, 14-year-old Kara Borden until the Pennsylvania detectives arrived. Nevertheless, the 6'3" 240-pounder learned some useful information from the young girl sitting before him, who was the subject of a nationwide Amber Alert.

Bridges was not technically interviewing Kara as a suspect, due to her age and her still-unresolved status as a possible victim, so he did not tape their conversation. He did however, take detailed notes.

Kara was clearly very upset, Bridges observed. Her arms were tightly wrapped around herself and she continually rocked back and forth in her seat as she cried. In between sobs she asked Bridges if he knew what was going on. He told her he didn't know, but that everything was going to be all right. Kara asked if "all this" was on national news, and Bridges replied again that he didn't know. She then asked what was going to happen to her, and how David was. Bridges assured her that she and her boyfriend would be okay. Bridges tried calming her by making small talk. Kara, according to the detective, was pretty much unresponsive, giving just one-word answers to his attempts to draw her into conversation.

Several minutes passed by in silence before Kara finally mentioned that they'd been in Indianapolis that morning trying to sell a $1,500 ring and bracelet, and how they were unsuccessful. Kara asked Bridges if she could watch TV and see how her family was. Bridges told her that he was sorry, but he couldn't permit it. Bridges knew, of course, that the murders were the lead story on all the news channels, and he didn't want Kara to hear from one of the dozens of TV journalists covering the case that her parents were dead. He left that thankless job to the Pennsylvania detectives, who were due in town any moment.

Kara explained that they had left Pennsylvania on Sunday at about 7:45 AM. She also told him that they had been refused a room the past evening and had to sleep in the cramped car on the side of the road, so they had no clue what was going on. Bridges nodded his head in understanding, but his hands were tied.

The next couple of hours the two chatted about her family and horses. She made a couple of visits to the bathroom. Bridges kept offering her food, knowing that the young girl hadn't eaten anything all day. Earlier she had even refused pizza that had been delivered.

The Department of Justice jet carrying the Lancaster policemen touched down at the Indianapolis International Airport around 5:30 PM. As it taxied into a private arrival area of the sprawling airport, a white-knuckled

Ed Tobin peeked out his window to see several Indiana State Police cruisers waiting for them on the tarmac. No sooner had they set foot on terra firma than they piled into two of the cruisers and sped off in the direction of nearby I-70, sirens blaring and lights flashing. An hour later, they pulled into the parking lot of the trooper barracks in Belleville.

At 6:30 PM they made official notification to Kara that her parents were dead. Detective Ed Tobin said there was no reaction from her, "no tears, no nothing." Tobin guessed that she had already known, or that she had figured it out for herself. Since the newly arrived detectives were more interested in talking to David Ludwig at this time, Kara was left in the care of Detective Bridges.

Interviewing Kara presented some problems, DA Totaro had warned the detectives. Because she was a minor, it was agreed that an interview had best wait until all were back in Lancaster and Kara was properly accompanied by a guardian.

Kara began crying again. She told Bridges she wanted to tell him what had happened the day before at her house. Bridges said, "If it makes you feel better." Bridges told her that because she was a minor, this was not an official police interview.

Kara related that she had met David about six months ago through mutual friends, and they had begun dating about six weeks ago. About a month ago she thought that David had gotten her pregnant, and they'd talked about running away, but it was a false alarm. She told Bridges that she had snuck out of her house this past Saturday night and into David's bedroom at his parents' house. When she'd tried getting back into her home at about 5:30 AM Sunday, her mom had caught her. An argument with her mother had ensued, which her father joined in on. Her parents kept demanding to know who she'd been with. At first Kara refused to tell, but her father threatened to call each one of her friends and ask them, thereby embarrassing her. Kara relented and told them. She also told them about their text-messaging communications when she would return home from his house. Kara claimed that her dad had taken her cell phone and intercepted David's call, telling him he had better come over and talk.

Kara said she had talked to David on their cell phones before he came over. He told her, she claims, "I'm coming over to get you, and I'm bringing my guns."

After David talked to her dad, she related, they got up and walked toward the front door. When she saw David draw his gun out of his pants, she began to run out of the kitchen to the backyard. She heard the two gunshots. She continued to run as fast as she could through the neighborhood until she eventually saw David's car on Rudy Dam Road. He was stopped and yelling for her. She abruptly ended her story at that point. It was now 10 PM and Bridges turned custody of Kara back over to Sergeant Warczynski. Kara was taken to a motel in nearby Cloverdale, where she spent the evening sharing a room with a female officer, a posted guard at her door and an unmarked patrol car in the parking lot. The next day, she would be flown back to Pennsylvania to be reunited with what remained of her family.

Belleville, a rural farming community, didn't have much in the way of amenities. The one and only motel—where Kara was also staying—and a local diner, however, were all the four lawmen from Pennsylvania needed. None of them could remember what they ate, and the rooms were spartan, but had beds. The last few days had exhausted them all, so they retired for the evening right after dinner. With David Ludwig in custody, all four slept as if they didn't have a care in the world.

ELEVEN

Search Warrants

The network's 24/7 news shows had been schooling like sharks around the Warwick police headquarters since Sunday morning. There was blood in the water and each program was diligently trying to outshine the other with scoops. The Borden murders and the Amber Alert for Kara had made it the crime *du jour* among the super-competitive news outlets.

The media coverage of the crimes "was a circus," said Detective Joe Geesey. The local media jostled for attention amongst the heavyweights from New York in fear of being scooped by the outsiders. The massive trailers and dish trucks assembled en masse in the parking lot of the Warwick Township police head-quarters, leaving little room for anybody else. Their wagon train of trucks extended out of the parking lot and another half mile down Clay Road. All the news-men were trying to find someone who would talk to them, making it a free-for-all.

Most policemen, says Geesey, don't have the experience to handle it, explaining "You have to be careful what you say to the media, the wrong thing broadcasted on the public airwaves might jeopardize the case."

"It is an adversarial relationship," said the gray-haired cop, ". . . since the media are trying to get as much information as possible and broadcast it out to the public, but they have no responsibility to the legal system, unlike the police, who do." On the other hand, Geesey knew, getting the word out on the missing teenagers, and the Amber Alert over the airwaves was an invaluable tool. He knew the authorities walked a fine line. Ed Tobin, never comfortable in front of a microphone or camera, breathed a sigh of relief when it was decided that only Chief Garipoli would address the media inquiries and dispense information cleared beforehand by DA Totaro's office. That freed Tobin and Geesey to focus solely on the investigation.

On Monday afternoon an aspect of the case was revealed that gave it a pop culture twist, which the media was quick to pounce on. Internet geeks found David and Kara's websites and blogs, and quickly spread the word. It was an aspect of the story that would further engross the viewing public, who had been watching the drama unfold on TV.

In an interview with Sam Lohr, Detectives Eric Zimmerman and John Schofield had learned that David and Kara often communicated secretly not only by text messaging on their cell phones, but also on the Internet using the popular web journal site Xanga.com. Lohr said he often communicated with his friend David this way, and that David used the screen name *Haydren* and Kara signed in as *karebear000*.

Four hours after talking with Sam, the MCFU executed a second search warrant on the Ludwig home in Lititz and seized two Hewlett-Packard laptops, a MultiWave desktop computer and an HP Palm Pilot. Sam

Lohr also turned over a laptop the next day that he said he had borrowed from David.

A separate search warrant was executed by Detective Chris Erb, a member of the Pennsylvania State Police (PSP) Computer Crimes Task Force, so he and Detective Pete Savage, Lancaster County DA's Office, and Jim Strosser of the PSP could conduct a preliminary preview forensic exam of the stored media/data on David's computers.

Chris Erb, 38 years of age, had been a computer forensic detective for over three years. His certifications and educational accomplishments filled an entire page of the official court record on the case. His qualifications were indisputable: they have never been challenged by a defense team in front of the bench. Although the detective is with the Lancaster City Bureau of Police, he is also a member of the Pennsylvania State Police Area I Computer Crimes Task Force.

The Area I Task Force—the state is split into five areas—is made up of some twenty detectives from different departments whose jurisdiction covers eleven counties in the Commonwealth, including Lancaster.

The district attorney's office called in Erb on November 14 to take part in the investigation. It was hoped that there might be some kind of electronic communication indicating where David Ludwig and Kara were heading or where they were.

"We wanted to assist them [the case investigators] in quickly tracking them down," said Erb, "and also to obtain anything of evidentiary value involving this case."

The storage media has to be examined in a "forensically sound environment," in this case, the forensic

lab on the third floor of the Lancaster City Bureau of
Police. State Police Trooper James Strosser and county
Detective Peter Savage joined Erb in the lab and split
the work. There was plenty to go around.

As a matter of procedure, the hard drives and memory chips have to be removed from the devices. Information cannot be removed from booting up the device
for fear of tainting the retrieved evidence.

The hard drives are placed in what is called a "write-
protected device." This device would allow detectives
to retrieve information from the drive and prohibit any
kind of writing to the drive.

From the write-protected device, Erb and his colleagues were able to obtain an exact image of the
drive. Then these images were loaded from the write-
protected device into a forensic computer, and a series
of evidence files were created and broken down into
chunks, resulting in a byte-by-byte copy of the actual
drive from the suspect computer.

These image files are then loaded into forensic soft-
ware that allows the detectives to do a complete and
thorough analysis of the information that is stored on
the suspect drive. That would include what is called a
"data carving."

A data carving is any material that may have
been deleted by the user. Contrary to popular belief,
"deleted" material is not actually removed from the
drive when the user hits the delete button, but placed
instead into a "drive-free space," or "unallocated space"
of the hard drive.

Essentially, when someone deletes a file on a computer, the data contained in the file does not actually

disappear—rather that data remains on the hard drive in an area unreachable by the user, until it is overwritten by new data. Therefore, deleted files, or remnants of deleted files, can remain in a computer free space, the "slack space"—for long periods of time before they are overwritten by new files.

When a user is connected to the Internet, simply viewing content from websites causes all the viewed content, text and image files to be saved to the hard drive. This viewed content is typically saved to what is called a cache folder, and it is also recoverable. In addition, a computer operating system may also keep a record of deleted data in a "swap" or "recovery" file. Thus, the ability to retrieve residue of an electronic file from a hard drive depends less on when the file was downloaded or viewed than on a particular user's operating system, storage capacity and computer habits.

Because of the urgency of the situation, Chris Erb ran a "preview" of the drives. The preview would allow the detectives to locate and see just the active files on a drive in a write-protected fashion. The preview to find something pertinent took several hours. Between the three men, several hundred hours went into this case.

Kara's computer was also reviewed by Detective Erb for personal contacts, and every individual whose name appeared was identified and eventually interviewed either in person or on the phone.

Most computer users, even many of the computer-savvy, don't realize that when they delete a file it can easily be recovered months or even years after it has been downloaded, saved onto a hard drive, deleted or viewed on the Internet. It is simply a matter of using readily available forensic tools.

The trio found that Ludwig had also maintained two other screen names, which were determined to be handles on AOL Instant Messenger and Yahoo Instant Messenger.

While conducting the forensic exam of the computer hard drives, Detective Erb found 398 items of evidentiary interest, many of them "flirtatious messages and inappropriate images" of David Ludwig and Kara Borden. Some of the images showed the two in various stages of undress. There were also stored images of David and friends brandishing firearms and swords.

Erb found a website belonging to David on MySpace.com where there was an adoring post from nonya that was signed "Kara." The computer forensic team knew they would need more "relevant material" from the servers to complete the computer tech investigation.

District Attorney Totaro's office contacted the legal department at MySpace in California and asked that they provide all relevant documents. They were very willing to comply, but indicated they needed a court order before they could do so. Rather than send a court order, Totaro contacted the Los Angeles County District Attorney's Office and asked if they would serve a search warrant on MySpace for the records. They agreed, the search warrant was served and the documents were promptly forwarded to the Lancaster District Attorney's Office.

The DA's office had more difficulty making contact with Xanga. Detective Geesey, who was the DA's in-house chief investigator, had to call the Manhattan district attorney's office to see if they could assist in locating the Xanga.com business facility or a representative of the company. The Manhattan DA's office was quick to respond, and they were able to make contact with Xanga. As a result, a search warrant was forwarded to the New York DA's office, and they served that warrant on Xanga. Shortly thereafter the documents were forwarded to the Lancaster DA's office.

The information that was requested were e-mail addresses, IP logs, dates and times of log-in, subscriber information and any and all Private Messages in the user's Inbox, Trash and Sent Mail.

Another search warrant was issued to Verizon Wireless of Pennsylvania for account information on the two teenagers' cellular phones, and records of all text messages between them. Totaro concluded his request by adding all the above "will further the investigation by providing information concerning the identities of those involved in this criminal activity and their method and manner of operation."

At the same time the police were seizing the computers, Lieutenant Ed Tobin was going through the arduous process of cataloging all the guns in the Ludwig residence in Lititz. There were fifty-nine of them. Police decided to remove them all from the Ludwig home in case David returned undetected.

The large number of firearms included just about every type imaginable: assault rifles, large- and small-caliber handguns, various gauge shotguns—pump and semiautomatic—hunting rifles with scopes, .22-caliber target rifles and thousands of rounds of ammunition. It was enough to arm a small cadre of guerrilla fighters, and it gave credence to the rumor circulating that Mr. Ludwig and family were preparing for Armageddon.

TWELVE

Arraignment

Indiana's Hendricks County Prosecutor Patricia Baldwin said David Ludwig had signed documents at the county jail that cleared the way for Tobin and Geesey to take him to face murder charges back in Lancaster. Baldwin said he could be returned to Pennsylvania as early as Tuesday, November 15.

Ludwig never considered fighting extradition. If he had, Totaro would have obtained the necessary governor's warrant. Although the formal process would have delayed his return to Pennsylvania, said Totaro, "it would have just been a matter of time."

On November 15, at 2:30 PM, Kara boarded the U.S. Department of Justice's jet for her ride back to Lancaster, accompanied by Geesey and Tobin. The hour-long flight was a quiet one.

Chief Garipoli described Kara as being a "mess" when police finally had her in custody, saying, "There's a fourteen-year-old child out there, crying a lot and devastated too. I don't think police are asking her anything."

Upon deplaning, she was quietly and quickly, and

with no fanfare, hustled into town to the county court-house Victim Services Unit.

Half an hour later the Indiana State Police prop plane carrying David Ludwig and escorts Detective Kerry Sweigart and FBI Agent Jeff Blaney landed at Lancaster Airport.

Sweigart and Ludwig conversed for the whole ninety-minute flight home. A friendly conversationalist, the East Cocalico detective found David Ludwig to be "a bright kid, well-spoken, calm and friendly." They talked about David's background and his interests: church and God, homeschooling, his job, how he wanted to study to be a nurse, how he had flown all over the world with his dad, who was a commercial pilot, and how he wanted to learn to fly—and, of course, hunting. He also asked Sweigart about Kara and where she was and how she was doing. He assured the "subdued" teen that she was headed home too and that she was fine.

At one point, about halfway through the flight, there was something David asked that Sweigart will never forget.

Ludwig had looked down at his manacled hands, paused for a moment of thought, looked back up at the 40-year-old cop and thoughtfully asked, "Detective Sweigart, do you think I'll ever get out of prison?"

"David, that isn't looking too good for ya now," was all he replied.

It was difficult to square with reality that this "nice kid" had calmly shot two innocent people to death. Kerry Sweigart thought this, like most homicides, didn't have to happen. Now, not only were two people dead, but young lives were ruined—and all in just a few seconds of unbridled emotion.

Sweigart felt terrible telling the teenager the reality of the situation: that there was little hope he would ever be free again to go to school, hunt or fly. Sweigart was a father too, and David's fate saddened him. The two resumed their conversation about their interests.

Ed Tobin had foreseen the security problems of bringing in the high-profile suspect to the small Warwick Township district judge's office. The media was expected to be at the arraignment en masse, with more warm bodies than the small office could safely accommodate. It had been pre-arranged to have Ludwig arraigned at the Lancaster County Courthouse, a large modern edifice in Lancaster City.

The county sheriff's department provided a fleet of vehicles to ensure that the transport would occur free of any incident. Two officers and a van, surrounded by squad cars with lights flashing, whisked Ludwig away to his rendezvous with District Judge Daniel B. Garrett, who was awaiting the suspect in a borrowed Commonwealth judge's courtroom on the third floor of the courthouse.

At 4 PM the van entered the exit ramp of the underground garage to avoid the media horde, then took the wanted felon on an elevator to the third floor. The courtroom was overflowing with reporters craning their necks to get a look at the tall, handsome teen who was accused of shooting two innocent people to death. The media was still speculating whether he was a modern day Romeo or a cold-blooded murderer in the mold of Charlie Starkweather.

Tobin had a formal copy of the warrant, which he served on Ludwig. The detective explained to Ludwig that he was being charged with two counts of criminal homicide and kidnapping. In Pennsylvania the accused is required to read the face of the warrant. Once read, Ludwig was asked by Tobin if he understood the charges against him. Ludwig nodded his head and said yes. The veteran detective, who had seen his share of scared and confused prisoners, was impressed with Ludwig's calm and stoic demeanor—this, for a kid who must have known by then that he would be facing the death penalty.

Judge Garrett clarified the information on the warrant, as per procedure, asking him his name, date of birth and home address. He also asked again if he understood the charges against him, and again David Ludwig answered yes.

Judge Garrett informed the handcuffed Ludwig that since there was no bail granted for defendants charged with murder in the Commonwealth of Pennsylvania, he was being remanded to the fortress-like Lancaster County Prison. The whole procedure lasted no more than ten minutes.

Two sheriff's deputies then took custody of the prisoner and transported him over to the prison, his home for the next seven months.

THIRTEEN

The Funeral

Gary Crow, Cathy's brother, who lived in Harrisburg, handled the care of the younger children and the legal problems with Kara, with the help of the two older boys, Justin and Jamie. Gary's home, 40 miles from Lititz, became the base from which the extended family operated and made funeral arrangements. Except for the media, the outpouring of help and support from the community was great, Steven related.

The funeral for the slain couple was held at the Lancaster Bible College's chapel in Lancaster on Saturday morning, November 19, six days after the murders. The turnout was huge, with hundreds of people cramming into the cavernous building. Catherine Hart related that many Cadmus retirees, employees from other company plants and customers were in attendance. The media were kept off the property, but lined the roads leading up to the Fundamentalist Christian college.

At the funeral a family friend, Kellymarie Conlon, told reporters that the Bordens' ". . . faith informed every aspect of their lives. And in their time of grief, faith has given their children a lifeline. Michael and

Cathryn raised a family that's very devout in their faith, and their faith is holding them up."

Elders from Monterey Bible Chapel led a funeral service with a strongly evangelistic tone. There was little mention of the tragedy. None of the Bordens' five children spoke during the service. Kara Borden, wearing a light-colored sweater, sat with her four siblings during the funeral. Since returning from Indiana, she had been in seclusion with her brothers and sister and had made no statements to the press. At the public service, the Borden kids appeared, according to news reports, "drawn but composed," even as they greeted mourners two hours later.

Rex Trogden, the Bordens' friend and church minister in North Carolina, said in his eulogy that, "I'd like to introduce you to the word 'triumph.'" He said it was a hard word to speak when standing on a stage behind two closed caskets, with five orphaned children in the front row.

"They risked their lives together," Trogden said. "Mike and Cathy were willing not only to risk their lives, but to lay down their lives. And they did so . . . together."

Trogden referred to the funeral as a "home-going to be with the Lord."

"They loved you so much," he said, speaking to the Borden children, "and cared for you so well, and prayed for you."

Trogden said that "Mike" had a "wonderfully dry sense of humor." He related how on one Christmas, Cathy wanted the biggest tree they could find, to best display all the family ornaments. But the tree was so big that it had to be trimmed before it would fit into the house. For Christmas, Mike gave Cathy a crystal snowman with an inscription: "Room for one more ornament."

"It's difficult for us to say good-bye," fellow church elder Bill Bradford said in his benediction. "It should be easy to look forward to a time when we can say, 'Welcome home.'"

He quoted Matthew 5:4, "Blessed are those who mourn, for they will be comforted," and John 16:22, "Now is your time of grief, but I will see you again and you will rejoice, and no one will take away your joy."

"This," Rex Trogden said, "is not the end."

Afterward, the children and other family members attended a graveside service at Landis Valley Mennonite Cemetery.

Tina Shyver-Plank said she and her fellow employees were all in a state of shock after the news of Mike's death. A pervasive silence ruled that Monday after Mike's murder, with gathering groups hoping to hear more information. The Cadmus employees had a moment of silence in honor of him. A Borden family trust fund was established for the children. Everyone also wrote tributes in a book that was circulated around the company for the family. "Mike was one of the nicest people I ever met," Shyver-Plank said. "I will never forget him. There was a light around him. He was personable and caring, kind and gentle. We lost our leader, and everyone would tell you that it hurt. He made a shy girl smile—that's how I remember him most. I wrote an encouraging letter to his youngest son and sent him an angel pin that I had for years, but never took out of the package. I knew one day that it would find its rightful owner."

Michael Borden's picture hangs framed in the lobby, and the stately main conference room is named after him.

Tom Mannon and his wife and daughters were neighbors and friends who lived a few doors down from the Bordens. He said on an MSNBC report that the Bordens were ". . . a very, very nice family, you know, great to have them as neighbors. We've known them for about nine years, and of course my two daughters, being about the Bordens' daughters' ages, have, you know, struck up friendships with them over the years."

The Bordens had employed a local girl, Reba Zimmerman, to help Mrs. Borden with the housekeeping chores, since she was often busy teaching her kids at home. On CBS-TV, Zimmerman added, ". . . everyone in the area is very shocked, simply knowing the Bordens as a very kind, loving family. In this community, nothing like this ever happens."

Zimmerman, however, refused to talk about the Bordens later, saying that they were a private family and she wanted to respect that. She would only say that the Bordens were "everybody's neighbors" and they "were nice ones." She said she only appeared on TV because Kara was, at that point, still missing, and she wanted to help get the word out on the Amber Alert for her, so "they wouldn't find her dead body in a river later."

Neighbor Tom Mannon echoed that sentiment being expressed by family, friends and neighbors of the Bordens.

"I don't think it made sense to anyone," Mannon said on MSNBC-TV. "And while we all have questions at this point, we're getting a bit weary of all the, you know, intrusion, and hope that it, you know, comes to a conclusion pretty quickly."

The siblings of both Michael and Cathryn Borden refused all requests to comment on the tragedy, and were shielded by lawyers. Probably more perplexing was the fact that no one from the Bordens' church, the Monterey Bible Chapel in Leola, stepped forward to comment on what must have been a tragedy for the small Fundamentalist church, especially since Michael Borden was a church elder.

For the last two years, on the anniversary of his death, Tina Shyver-Plank has put a rose on his and his wife's grave in honor of them. She is not the only one.

Kevin Eshleman is the executive pastor at the nearby Ephrata Community Church (ECC), another of the Christian Fundamentalist churches that seem to thrive in Lancaster County. Kara and older sister Katelyn attended some of his church's youth group meetings. He was bombarded by media requests for information, since his church's connection to Kara was mentioned in one of her Internet blogs. Unlike the Monterey Bible Chapel (MBC) the ECC has a phone listing and a paid staff that maintains office hours.

"The Bordens attended the Monterey Chapel," said Eshleman, who knows only a little about the small, mysterious sect, "and the church is a fairly small, conservative congregation that believes in what we call in these parts a 'free ministry,' which is similar to the Mennonite, Brethren and Amish congregations."

The Monterey Chapel does not have a paid ministry staff. Only the members seem to know who their leaders are and when they meet. They publish no contact information, simply a listed meeting place.

Even though the MBC is located in heavily Amish Leola, the MBC is distinct from the Amish. Eshleman says the "flavor" of the MBC is different. The MBC congregation has different expressions or styles of worship, and a different structure. They, however, share many of the same values with the Amish.

The church elders exercise oversight of the congregation. This leadership team usually consists of four or five men who take turns preaching and executing leadership responsibilities. Michael Borden was one of those leaders. Eshleman heard it was a "good place" and it was "nothing like a cult or any such thing." The church simply operated differently from the ECC and most other traditional churches.

There certainly was nothing traditional about how they handled the Borden murders. It was almost as if it were a conspiracy of silence regarding anything about the Bordens by those who knew them. It was a bit disingenuous, since the silence only increased interest in the private religious couple's lives and their church. It would add fuel to the burning mystery of who these people were.

Trogden says his church is "non-denominational," with its main message being the Gospel, "that is, that Christ died for the sins of the world, was buried and raised again."

The BBC, says the church elder, is also a small—100 members—Christian Fundamentalist congregation. There are several other churches associated with the BBC, but in a non-denominational structure. The BBC doesn't have a church government that is located someplace else that legislates for them. The BBC is strictly independent, and the Monterey Bible Chapel, says Trogden, is "just like them."

His divinity school training was, as he says with a laugh, "on-the-job training." In 1992 the Christians at the BCC gathered there in fellowship and recognized the "commendation" of Trogden to do the "Lord's work."

Rex Trogden says that in his church—contrary to popular belief—women are every bit equal to the male church members. "For the record," Trogden said, "we do not have women preachers, mainly because the Bible says that women don't have that role or service." He adds that in no way does the preaching ban minimize their role or quality. They are men's complete equals.

Reverend Trogden gave the eulogy at the Bordens' funeral at Lancaster Bible College. Unlike his northern brethren in Leola, Trogden was willing to talk about his friends and fellow churchmen, the Bordens.

Trogden first met Mike and Cathy in Charlotte when he returned from a mission for the church in Zaire—now the Congo—in 1996. He and his wife were happy to be back home after ten years in the poor third-world country. The Bordens had joined the church in his absence.

The contact Rex Trogden had with Mike and Cathy Borden was almost entirely through the church on Sunday mornings, which the churchman admits is not much "in the way of developing a relationship." The two families had an occasional meal together, sometimes at the Bordens' home, sometimes at the Trogdens'. When the Bordens moved north, Trogden was often invited to the little church in Leola to preach to their congregation, and shared some meals with them when he was there.

He found the Bordens to be wonderful people. Trogden says they were a "normal family, had a happy home with children that were glad to be part of the family, that joined in on the conversations around the dinner table."

The key interest that they enjoyed talking about was "the things in the Bible."

"There was nothing abnormal about the conversations," says Trogden. "It wasn't anything far-flung, fanatical or strange, like a lot of people might look for in what happened in their [the Bordens'] lives." Rather it was "just taking a good understanding in what the Bible teaches in a good, happy way."

The Bordens apparently had a very good marital relationship. Mike was not domineering, with Cathy being an equal, very much an active participant in conversation and in her parenting role. Says their friend Trogden, "they were both in there together."

Trogden was caught completely off-guard and genuinely shocked at the murders of his friends, and at Kara's running off with the murderer/boyfriend. He was never aware of any sign of discord between parent and child. "They were a happy Christian family."

Aerial photo of the Borden home (second row, middle house) on the day of the murders.   *Courtesy of the Warwick Township PD*

15 Royal Drive, where Michael and Cathy Borden were murdered.
Courtesy of the Warwick Township PD

Best friends Kayla Jeffries and Kara Borden.
Courtesy of Kayla Jeffries

Kayla Jeffries was the case investigators' "go-to girl."
Courtesy of Kayla Jeffries

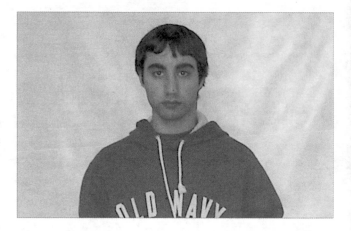

Mug shot of Sam Lohr.
Courtesy of the Warwick Township PD

Front door of the Borden home, where Michael Borden was shot.
Courtesy of Kevin F. McMurray

The VW Jetta after it was forced off the road by the Indiana troopers. David is sitting beside the car handcuffed.
Courtesy of Indiana State Police

The interior of the VW Jetta after the crash with David visible through the doors. *Courtesy of Indiana State Police*

Trooper Dave Cox was the first to spot the Amber Alert VW Jetta.
Courtesy of Indiana State Police

Trooper Dave Furnas engaged Ludwig in the dangerous high-speed pursuit.
Courtesy of Indiana State Police

East Cocalico PD Sergeant
Larry Martin.
Courtesy of Larry Martin

East Cocalico PD Detective
Kerry Sweigart.
Courtesy of Kerry Sweigart

David Ludwig in the custody of the Indiana State Police the day
after his capture. *Courtesy of Indiana State Police*

The historic Lancaster County Jail.

Courtesy of Kevin F. McMurray

Indiana State Police Lieutenant Detective Jeffery Hearon took Ludwig's confession.
Courtesy of Indiana State Police

Warwick Township PD Detective Eric Zimmerman.
Courtesy of Kevin F. McMurray

Detective Joe Geesey (left) and District Attorney Don Totaro.

Courtesy of Kevin F. McMurray

Lieutenant Detective Ed Tobin (left) and Detective Joe Geesey led the Borden homicide investigations.

Courtesy of the Warwick Township PD

Defense attorney and death penalty opponent Merrill Spahn.
Courtesy of Kevin F. McMurray

FOURTEEN

Protecting Kara

Robert "Bob" Beyer was retained by the Borden family, headed now by Michael's brother David, in conjunction with Justin and James, the two grown sons of Michael and Cathryn. Beyer would represent Kara in all the legal proceedings. To make it official, Kara's uncle gave the lawyer a one-dollar bill. Beyer was impressed with Kara's brother and sister and her aunts and uncles, calling them "real stand-up people who Kara was lucky to have."

The court had already appointed a legal guardian, Joanne Murphy. Murphy spent a few minutes with Kara alone to introduce herself, and for Kara to get comfortable with her. Murphy also explained the reasons for the temporary guardianship.

Coincidentally Beyer was involved, peripherally, in the events that had culminated in the shooting death by police of wanted felon Daniel Faust just the week before the murders of the Bordens. Faust had shot the Lititz cop who'd tried to arrest him on a misdemeanor warrant, and then fled the scene.

One of Faust's relatives had called Beyer shortly after the cop was shot and wanted the lawyer to arrange a peaceful surrender of the wanted man. It seems Faust feared that he would be beaten by the cops when taken into custody, in revenge for the shooting of their fellow officer. Beyer quickly contacted DA Totaro, Lieutenant Ed Tobin and two other county detectives and told them Faust would surrender himself to two of the older detectives, Ed Tobin and Detective Jan Walters, whom Beyer knew would not harm him.

The information was in the process of being relayed to Faust when he was killed. There was a shootout with law enforcement, in what all law enforcement agreed was a "suicide by cop." Beyer would later represent Faust's aunt in a case of obstruction of justice and the hindering of the apprehension of a felon. The woman got off with a probationary sentence.

Beyer met Kara for the first time in DA Don Totaro's office at 6 PM, once Kara arrived at the office from the airport. Geesey and Tobin were also present. Beyer first spent an "hour or two" with her "not to get information out of her," he explained, "but just to get to know each other, so as she could trust him."

For the integrity of the investigation, after speaking with Kara in private, Beyer informed the district attorney that he didn't think kidnapping was an issue. According to Beyer, DA Totaro didn't seem surprised at the defense attorney's contention. He agreed with Beyer, expressing his personal belief that Kara hadn't been abducted by force. Beyer assumed Totaro had come to that conclusion, since David Ludwig had now been interviewed twice and Totaro had David's statements proclaiming Kara's innocence in the murders of her parents. There were also the statements of her brother and sister taken by police right after the shootings.

Totaro's office was unusually busy, and because of the sensationalism the case was generating, the DA was reluctant to throw one of his inexperienced Assistant District Attorneys (ADAs) into the media maelstrom. He decided to handle this one himself.

Despite the notoriety the case got, Beyer, himself a former ADA in Lancaster for five years, was somewhat surprised that Don Totaro would personally try the case. Beyer had seen good trial lawyers get elected district attorney before and then find themselves, much to their chagrin, being administrators and not courtroom advocates. The county had grown too much and it needed all the attention of a managing district attorney. Apparently this case was the exception. Beyer knew what kind of prosecutor Totaro was: smart, aggressive and ambitious, with a good legal mind. He was not the type of prosecutor to settle—if he knew he had a potential felon, he prosecuted. In his client's case, Beyer had never seen such a comprehensive investigation of a homicide.

Due to the late hour, everyone involved was exhausted, and since Kara was now considered a victim, Beyer suggested that the interview wait until morning. Totaro, Geesey and Tobin had no objection. Because of her minor status, Kara spent the evening in the county juvenile center, but, as attorney Beyer made clear, not as a "delinquent child," but as a "dependent child," so she didn't have to spend the night in "the bad kids' wing." She had her own room in the dependents' wing.

Detectives Joe Geesey, Ed Tobin and Peter Savage

finally got a chance to interview Kara at the Youth Intervention Center early the next morning. Sitting beside her were her court-appointed guardian Joanne Murphy and attorney Bob Beyer.

Geesey wanted to find out if the petite blonde teenager was complicit in the murder of her parents. The veteran detective was particularly interested in her phone conversations with Ludwig the morning of the shootings, after she had been caught trying to sneak back into the house. Beyer continuously walked out of the room with Kara so he could advise her privately before answering a question.

Beyer later said that, had it been an investigator other than Joe Geesey, the continual lawyer/client private consultations might not have been necessary. Geesey's questioning was, in the opinion of the defense attorney, "inappropriate."

Geesey believed he was only doing his job. The two men had clashed before on other cases and were not particularly fond of each other.

Kara, if she was withholding information about her part in the deaths of her parents, might have been tripped up by making statements that conflicted with what David Ludwig had confessed. Notable was David's claim that he'd warned Kara that if he came over, he might have to shoot her parents.

When she came back in the room after a consultation with Beyer, she was careful about how her admissions were stated, very deliberate in not agreeing with Ludwig's assertions or implicating herself in any conspiracy. Despite the shielding from her attorney, Geesey would later say that he thought Kara was a cold and calculating young woman, and that she was "damn smart."

The meeting lasted almost three hours and, despite the trauma she suffered and the fact that what Kara had undergone was all beginning to sink in, she had handled herself quite well, Beyer believed.

Attorney Beyer and the Borden family were upset that once the kidnapping charges against David Ludwig were unofficially dropped, the DA's office added sexual assault charges. The implication being, of course, that Kara had been seduced by David Ludwig, four years her senior. It was an unfair characterization of the young girl, because as Beyer was always quick to say about his client, she was a victim.

Since they had Ludwig's confessions to two murders, Beyer questioned, why was Kara being made the victim again? Beyer guessed that the sexual charges against Ludwig would be effective "aggravators" (as opposed to mitigators) in getting him sentenced to death, even at the expense of Kara's now-suspect reputation.

The media immediately began to attack and distort Kara's sexual behavior. For example, they favored the use of the Internet-posted photo of her wearing a red headband that made her look like a "trollop." It was hard to find published photos of her looking like the girl next door, which was a more accurate portrayal of her, Beyer insisted. Instead, Beyer said, they made her look like "some tramp straight out of *Desperate Housewives.*"

Beyer, good defense attorney that he is, was fairly successful in casting Kara as a victim. The sexual charges brought against Ludwig, in some press accounts, made her appear to be a victim rather than a co-conspirator in her parents' deaths. This, of course, was exactly what Beyer wanted, since there was a jury pool out there that was likely closely following the case.

The Borden family denied media requests to interview Kara and to get her story. Through attorney Beyer, they turned down the reigning queen of daytime TV, Oprah Winfrey, several times. ABC-TV's Diane Sawyer, CNN's Catherine Crier and a plethora of other media notables were all rebuffed. This after many of them made substantial offers of money and college scholarships to get the exclusive interview with a real-life Juliet. Kara, like her parents and their killer, was proving to be an enigma.

One person who knew the two young Borden girls and would speak of them, was Pastor Kevin Eshleman of the Ephrata Community Church (ECC).

Kara, her sister Katelyn and some of her friends had come to participate in one of the Ephrata Community Church's youth groups, which, according to Eshleman, was a bit "irregular," since they were not church members. The Borden girls had come to the group with some fellow homeschoolers in their network who belonged to the ECC.

The group was putting on a back-to-school party, and it was mentioned in one of Kara's Internet blogs, which the media picked up on when the story broke. Eshleman was immediately bombarded with interview requests.

According to Eshleman, the ECC, out of the three churches mentioned in connection with the case—the two others being the Monterey Bible Chapel and the Lititz Christian Church—knew the least about the Bordens and Ludwigs. "But we were listed in the phone book," Eshleman said.

The Ephrata church pastor had met Michael and Cathryn Borden just once when they had come to pick up Kara and Katelyn. Eshleman made a point of saying hello to the parents just as a way of introducing himself, so they would at least know who he was in case they had any questions about what the group was doing.

Katelyn, said the ECC pastor, seemed to have her "head together." She knew what she was doing and where she was going. Katelyn appeared to be "wise and not flighty, and a bit cautious," unlike so many girls her age. Kara was just as intelligent, but more carefree and friendly than her sister.

Initially Kara was friendly with everybody. She certainly was not "boy crazy," said the Ephrata minister. But six months before the murders, Kevin Eshleman did see a change in the pretty young teen. The pastor, who had been involved in youth ministry for many years, noticed that Kara had developed some "negative influences" in her life, and as a result, began to pull away from the youth group.

Eshleman asked her friend Carissa, who expressed the same concern for Kara. Something was definitely stirring, but had just not surfaced yet. It was a perceptional thing with the minister. It was not like he'd caught her smoking cigarettes or drinking, or anything that would demonstrate dilemmas for the girl. He said he saw no concrete signs that "we have a problem here."

Since Kara was not part of his congregation, Eshleman did not feel it was his place to bring the attitude change to the attention of her parents or even to discuss it with Kara. As the teenager already had a "home church" and her parents were "believers," he felt he would have been intruding. If he'd had a more personal connection to the young girl, he certainly would have spoken to her and her parents.

The 43-year-old minister would later speculate that it was Kara's blossoming romance with David Ludwig and the problems it posed for her that were the reason for her shift in attitude.

FIFTEEN

The Internet Connection

Detective Erb and his computer forensic team attempted to stay under the media radar while providing valuable information for the district attorney. The press, however, got wind of the Internet connection from followers of the case, who quickly discovered the websites.

On his Xanga site, David appeared to be your typical teenager. His homepage listed his interests, which included:

Rock climbing, hanging out with friends, computers, movies, swimming, volleyball, dirtbiking, playing cards, eating candy, spending money, traveling, pulling stupid pranks, having soft air gun wars, and various other things.

Expertise: *Computers, volleyball, movies, getting in trouble:-p*

David Ludwig's last entry in expertise of "getting in trouble" intrigued many, but similar entries could be found on just about all teenage Internet journals. David grossly exaggerated his income from "computer sales" to the tune of $250,000.

In his last entry before the killings, there was no inkling of what was to happen on November 13. He wrote of his purchase of his third laptop.

The moral of the story . . . watch out, you never know when God will miraculously give you a sale . . . then blow your socks off with an even greater sale. Don't ever settle for the good when you can get the best! God bless guys!

On David Ludwig's Internet photo gallery, there are sixty-five pictures of himself alone, which seemed an indication of his self-absorbed personality. Twenty of the photos depict hunting scenes. Although much would later be read into the "violent images" of him wielding a sword, posing with kills and field-dressing a freshly killed deer, there was nothing on the sites that couldn't be found on thousands of others maintained by teenagers. David's interest in hunting would become an obsession for the TV talking heads, and a bottomless well for opinion writers to go to for more copy on the case.

On Kara's MySpace page, she is depicted in a posted snapshot as a pretty blonde-haired, brown-eyed girl in a pink top, carefully hiding her braces behind tight lips. She claimed to be 17 and listed talking on the phone, the beach, and soccer as her fun things to do in the brightly colored pink-lined black boxes on the page. The homeschooled high school-aged freshman also wrote, "Books are so gay."

The offensive comment, many thought, was a result of her fundamental religious upbringing, and also an instilled suspicion of traditional education.

Next to her picture was a quote: ". . . Cause I need you and miss you." Most ascribed the person she was referring to as David Ludwig, possibly a line from a favorite song. Kara also wrote about the bands she liked and about her baptism. The thread of their religion runs throughout both Kara and David's websites.

Kara's everyday life revolved around her church. One news report said that Kara was baptized in a backyard hot tub. She told her friends on her blog about it on October 4th:

> *most of you didnt know that i did get baptized on sunday..hah..yeah so for you at LCC that got baptized this summer..look what i got baptized in.*wicked grin*[sic]*

The night before she was baptized Kara went to David's blog at MySpace:

> **YAY* heh you have to leave me a comment babe!! k? mk byeeeeeee lyl <3Kara<3*

Kara and David went together to a Christian music concert in October just a month before the murders:

> *The concert last night was AMAZING!! Pillar and Audio A rock my face off!*

> *HEY guys!!! hehe wow the concert was awesome..PILLAR ROCKED!! i love them! sweetttt!!*

anddd i got a pillar sweatshirt..tis very hot . . .
[sic]

When police reported that David and Kara had disappeared, they described Kara wearing a Pillar sweatshirt.

The computer entries were a fascinating look into a subculture of Christian contemporary music and their personal search for Jesus. It's a place where music speaks volumes to the believers; especially, it seemed, to the Lancaster County homeschooled teens who rarely strayed out of their close-knit social circles.

In a stunning revelation on November 23, an instant message transcript of a chat Kara had had with another underaged friend on October 17, 2005 (four weeks before the murders), surfaced in the media. It appears Kara made a series of blogs that were posted on Xanga and MySpace, some under a variation of her handle *karebear.* The blog transcript reported by the *Lancaster New Era* showed a different side to the sweet, innocent, religious homeschooled teenager, and began to foster the belief that perhaps she was a co-conspirator in the murders of her parents.

The picture of Kara also didn't appear to be the same girl depicted on karebear's website. The one here looked like some brooding malcontent, wearing a baseball cap and sunglasses and flipping what looked like either a peace sign or a lewd gesture.

Her friend wrote that she worried about her, typing in:

Friend: this is my place. cuz no one else knows and things
are getting out of hand . . ."

Kara: why what do you know? . . . if it has to do with david
and me, we are taking care of it—so you are just gonna go
tell everyone?

Friend: no i'm not. i will NEVER do that . . .

Kara: whatever it is, just leave it alone. david and i have
enough to deal with.trust me.

Friend: trust you? umm no cuz you're both lying to me . . .

Kara: i dont want you to get involved in it. you have no
place.

Friend: well then you two should have thought about that
before you let this go any farther then liking each
other..

Kara: why are you even my friend. . . . see i have to act . . .

Kara's conversation with her friend did not end
well, with her screaming in computer-ese:

YOU DONT UNDERSTAND WE TOOK THAT RISK THE FIRST NIGHT
HE CAME OVER . . . we said you couldnt understand why we
took the risk . . . but why we liked eachother but (. . .)
you have no idea

Kara's friend said, abbreviating the word "whatever" as w/e,

I can understand someone liking someone, but w/e
Kara . . .

Kara Beth Borden seemed adamant:

you dont know [. . .] how much we want to be with each
other . . .

Friend:

whatever, "you dont know [. . .] how much we want to be
with each other . . ."

The article on the transcript in the *New Era* suggested that the relationship between David and Kara was "intense" and "sexual in nature," and was causing problems with at least one of her friendships. It seemed to suggest that Kara was also some kind of a Jekyll and Hyde.

But through all the threads and webpage postings, there is no hint of what would happen on November 13. There appears to be no indication of rage, anger or frustration.

It wasn't long after the discoveries of the sites by the curious that the blogs began.

David's page became a message board of its own, complete with advice, insults, wishes for damnation and capital punishment, and notes of sympathy. Website bloggers quickly dubbed the niche postings as "Ludwigpalooza." The site got over 20,000 messages.

In one fairly typical one, a female blogger in a message to the accused murderer wrote:

ON THE NEWS IT SAID U Were A CHRISTIAN MY ASS U
WOULDNT HAVE KILLED HER PARENTS IF U Were!!!!

One post included a "Free David" graphic and an invitation to join the "David Double Homicide Fan Club."

Kara's MySpace webpage didn't escape attention either. Blogs quickly clogged the inbox, so much so that a friend of Kara irately posted the following for Kara:

STOP SENDING ME MESSAGES JUST TO ASK QUESTIONS ABOUT
KARA. . . . SO MORE THAN LIKELY, YOU ARE WASTING YOUR
TIME SENDING ME ONE.

It didn't have much of an effect. The blogs continued until another friend took the site private and made it accessible only to her friends—but not before writing this missive:

Yes it true what happened, the muder [sic] and abduction—
as far as anything else . . . I am not sure at the moment. I
would greatly appriciate [sic] it if you ALL stopped messaging me and Kara and even David. Thanks for your prayers
-it's greatly appriciated [sic]!

SIXTEEN

Homeschooling

On MSNBC's *The Abrams Report* for November 14, the correspondent had a neighbor and friend of the Bordens, Tom Mannon, and a former FBI profiler Clint Van Zandt to provide some insight on the still-unfolding drama. It wasn't long before the subject of homeschooling came up.

MANNON: The boy was infatuated with Kara, that the commonality there was their homeschooling. And there was evidently some kind of bonding that really happened between them. And neither sets of parents wanted that to develop, and so you know they said it had come to a point where it has to end, and so they responded by doing it on the sly.

ABRAMS: And, Clint, what do you make of this notion that they met each other through homeschooling?

VAN ZANDT: Well, you know, I know a lot of people who homeschool their kids. You know, you do it for religious reasons. You do it because you don't want—you don't particularly want your kids exposed to some of the things you think may or may not be in the public school system. But you know the reality is, you know you can't hothouse your children.

They are still going to have social interactions, relationships. I think this may point out with this young man, somehow, Dan, he didn't have the ability to develop conflict resolution skills. He wasn't wearing a black raincoat. He wasn't a member of the, you know, Trench Coat Mafia . . . [referring to the garb the Columbine High School killers and their outcast buddies wore].

Diane Patton is the home school coordinator for the central office for the School District of Lancaster. Homeschooling is one of the "five hats" the administrator wears for the district.

Patton explains that when a parent decides to homeschool they, as far as the state of Pennsylvania is concerned, become their own school district. The required application to the state must go through the public school district they live in. A parent can choose to homeschool their child when the child reaches the age of 8 years. Neither the parent nor anyone in the household can have a felony conviction, and he or she must have at least a high school education. Defined curriculum hours, required testing and immunizations are all strictly monitored by the state and the neighborhood district. The parents, however, choose what they will use to teach the child—for example they can teach reading and writing out of a book on drama or art just as each school district in the county does. They can also teach the Christian Fundamentalist favorite Creationism, as opposed to the secular, science-backed Darwinism. The district and the state cannot mandate the content of the education, as long as the child is receiving the required curriculum hours.

If there is reason to believe that the student is not getting the required instruction, or is not being properly cared for, the district would send a certified letter requesting evidence from the parent that the child is receiving good care and a proper education. The parent is given several days to produce the evidence, and they also have the right to demand an official hearing.

At the end of every school year the parent must pay for an outside evaluator—usually a certified teacher—who looks at the student's portfolio and work accrued, and conducts a fifteen-minute interview with the student.

Patton says she has no legal right to ask parents why they choose homeschooling over the public schools, and even though she is reluctant to say it, conceding only that it is a "factor," one big reason in religion-steeped Lancaster County is the sizeable number of Christian Fundamentalists who reside there.

Homeschoolers, once they have finished their courses of study, do not receive a district diploma, credit or transcripts. They receive nothing. The parent, however, can request testing of the child to enable them to get a General Education Degree (GED).

Warwick Township School District Deputy Superintendent Dr. Robert Lombardo spoke in measured words about homeschooling, which he oversees for the district in Lititz and Warwick Township. Although to many it is clear that the preponderance of homeschooling in Lancaster is the result of Fundamental Christian values, Lombardo denies it. He cites Pennsylvania law that any citizen has the right to school their children at home, for whatever reason. Lombardo, like Diane Patton, can't even ask the parents why they want to opt out of the traditional schooling methods of the district. As long as they abide by regulations and the children are properly schooled by state standards, there is no reason for him to know the parents' motives.

Dr. Lombardo's reticence on the subject of Christian values and homeschooling may have a cause: No school official wants to stir up a controversy in the pious community, particularly one that involves sex and murder, the main two components in the David Ludwig case.

Lombardo estimates that in any given year, they have between 100 to 200 children being taught by a parent at home in lieu of sending the students off to a public school. The deputy superintendent says that he is on the record for stating that the homeschool parents of the Lititz community do a "fantastic job, by following all state guidelines, and the children do well." Lombardo also says that as far as the "mechanisms they choose, that is up to the families." He is, of course, alluding to textbooks and teaching techniques—i.e. communal teaching. It is telling that the official said of the Ludwig case—and the role of homeschooling in it— that it was a "sensitive subject."

Homeschooling's academic worth is heatedly debated by experts in the field. It is impossible to obtain a representative sample of homeschooled children, and researchers cannot say for certain whether these children would do better or worse in a public or private school. Comparison studies have shown that while some homeschoolers who have taken state-mandated tests score below average, a majority test above that mark.

Proponents and opponents also disagree on how well-adjusted homeschooled children are. Although it appears to be true that children who are homeschooled spend less time with same-age children and more time with adults and children of different ages, research cannot prove that homeschooling harms children's social or psychological development. On the contrary, these children often demonstrate better social adjustment than their traditionally schooled peers.

Pop-psychologist Dr. Phil tackled the "sensitive subject" on his popular TV program.

He said homeschooling can be "wonderful" for small children, but not so for teenage kids:

"Once kids get to high school, social development is important. They become more independent. They want to interact on their own. So they don't do well in a homeschool environment."

William Lassiter of the Department of Juvenile Justice and Delinquency Prevention, the Center for the Prevention of School Violence, North Carolina, says peer interaction is important to teens:

"A lot of focus on education today is on testing, and the reality of it is, going to school is an education in itself, just by socializing kids. And that's the one greatest lesson a student can get out of it. 'How do I interact with other people?' "

Dr. Kathleen M. Heide, Ph.D., Professor of Criminology at the College of Arts and Sciences, University of South Florida, specializes in adolescent violence, and agrees with Lassiter. Dr. Heide said that parents run the risk of isolating their children from the world. By homeschooling, parents are preventing kids from interacting with their peers and maturing normally as opposed to possibly making their children antisocial.

Kara's attorney Bob Beyer believes that the attempt to shield kids from the realities of life, such as sex and violence, through homeschooling is doomed to failure. Beyer says it is a particular problem that the Fundamentalist Christian homeschooling network has failed to grasp.

"They think that by homeschooling and by tightening the rope and making the world small, that they've got control. That is an act in futility," Beyer said.

Yet, homeschooling is rarely conducted in total isolation. Many families participate in homeschool support groups, Scouting, church and recreational activities, and other associations.

The U.S. Department of Education has carefully studied the pros and cons of homeschooling, being that it has been a particularly vexing problem that constantly has been discussed in the media and in political forums. They concluded there was no pervasive evidence that indicated homeschooled children were detrimentally isolated from society, nor did they become antisocial in abnormally large numbers.

Sam Lohr, like his friend David Ludwig, was homeschooled. His father, Brian Lohr, says his family was a "bit of an anomaly" when it came to homeschooling their kids. The problem he had noticed with Sam was that he always seemed bored with school and had minor infractions, like talking and not paying attention in class.

A lot of their friends homeschooled, and Brian and his wife thought it was worth trying. Brian said his son "blossomed" under his wife's tutelage. Linda was a trained musician, and Sam had always shown a talent in music and the arts himself. Sam and his sister Heidi went on to graduate from the Mason Dixon Homeschoolers Association. Sam was the first student of theirs to graduate with a degree in theater production. As part of his curriculum he had studied acting in places like Chicago, Barbados and London. "It was a wonderful experience," said his dad. Sam would later enter college to study film.

Brian Lohr said his family didn't fit into a homeschooling niche. Because they live in a vibrant community, the Lohrs have friends whose kids attend public and private schools as well as being homeschooled. There is a tendency, says Lohr, for each kind of schooling family to form their own prejudices about each other. But Brian Lohr encouraged his kids to experience diverse cultures, and believed it prepared them for the "real world."

Heidi Lohr, besides being homeschooled, took three courses at Lancaster Catholic High School and pitched for the softball team. Heidi received a degree from Lancaster Catholic High School and from their homeschooling group, and managed to win a college athletic scholarship for softball. She presently is studying to be a history teacher at Columbia Union College while pitching for the softball team.

Detective Larry Martin of the East Cocalico Township Police Department was part of the team that worked the Ludwig case. He is also a homeschooling parent and helped his wife, a former educator, teach their five children at home. His eldest son is a sophomore and has never attended a public or private school. Martin says that a lot of so-called experts who disparage homeschooling are "full of crap and don't know really what they are talking about."

That the homeschooled kids don't get plenty of interaction with their peers is just "flat-out wrong," says Martin. His kids get plenty of it, since they belong to a support group, or co-op. For instance, he says, his kids are into drama and, since neither he nor his wife knows the first thing about it, his kids, along with others in their co-op, got a drama coach. The co-op parents (110 in all) hired a retired drama teacher. He meets with the kids every Friday and Saturday and instructs them in the finer points of acting. He also teaches American and British literature. Periodically the group puts on a play.

Detective Martin's kids belong to a quiz team on Monday nights. They go to music lessons on Tuesday nights and on Wednesday nights they attend their church group meeting. A lot of the co-op kids, says Martin, take courses at the local community college.

According to Martin, the "so-called experts" think homeschooled kids live in cabins in the middle of the woods and hit the books seven days a week in their isolation. It couldn't be further from the truth, he says, adding that they get more opportunities to socialize then most realize.

Martin, however, says homeschooling is not the only way to go. "It's a personal decision," he said.

Initially, wanting to give their kids a solid grounding in basic skills such as reading and writing, and fearing that their children would get lost in the crowd, they planned on homeschooling for just the first two years, then have them attend the public school from the third grade on. But their children thrived in the homeschooling atmosphere, so he and his wife continued. It also fostered a bond between the mother and father and the youngsters, something they couldn't have achieved had they sent their kids off to school.

Speaking as a cop, Sergeant Martin offered his opinion from his years of experience, that homeschooled David Ludwig is a psychopath.

"If he had been in a private Catholic high school, a private Protestant high school or a public school the same thing [the murders] would have happened. He was just a bad kid who gave homeschooling a black eye."

If any one group got bad public relations from the tragic events that occurred at 15 Royal Drive on November 13, 2005 it was the Coalition of Homeschoolers Across Lancaster County (CHALC). David Ludwig was a member of CHALC at the time of the murders.

Inexplicably CHALC would not comment on the case, but did take time to e-mail the author the following note:

The case you are referring to is not a homeschool issue and therefore not within our focus of ministry. CHALC does not have a comment for you.

Sincerely,
The CHALC Board of Directors

According to CHALC, the Christian homeschooling movement began in the 1970s. It really took root in the eighties when Dr. James Dobson began to champion the idea on his radio program. In 1983 two attorneys, Mike Farris and Mike Smith, formed the Home School Legal Defense Association (HSLDA) to fight for parental rights to homeschool.

Although CHALC did not want to comment, the HSLDA was eager to be heard.

The HSLDA, headquartered in Purcelleville, Virginia, clearly states that it does not hold religious views of parent and student as a litmus test for membership and defense, and that all homeschoolers are welcome. In their Q & A on their website they write this:

> HSLDA's mission is to protect the freedom of all homeschoolers. Although our officers and directors are Christians, HSLDA membership is not limited to religiously based homeschoolers. We respect parents' rights to make the appropriate choices for the upbringing of their children. We have no agenda to make all public and home-based classrooms religious or conservative. Our primary objective is to preserve the fundamental right of parents to choose home education, free of overzealous government officials and intrusive laws. We do put on a national conference annually and invite the board members of state organizations with whom we have worked for many years. Most, if not all, of those organizations have Christian leaders, but many serve all homeschoolers regardless of religious affiliation, as we do.

But the religious bent of the association is clearly evident from this passage found on their website:

All truth is God's truth. Man's knowledge is limited. We think we know something only to find that future generations have found that we really didn't know what we are talking about.

The truth is that God created the family. It is God's view of the family that is reflected in our western civilization and in our law until very recently. If we tear down this God-based view of the family, then all of the God-based principles in our society are ultimately at risk.

The reason we have parental rights is because our law assumes that God gave children to parents, not the state. If we eliminate the assumption of God from our law, parental rights and human rights themselves are impossible.

Because David Ludwig and Kara Borden were homeschooled, the HSLDA followed the case closely. Stating their willingness to defend the homeschooling ethos, they wrote:

Our communications goal regarding mainstream media is simply to promote, honestly and fairly, the merits of home education, for the good of homeschoolers universally.

The HSLDA is technically an association of member families. There are 80,000 dues-paying families, but there is no "group" that is formally associated with the legal defense association. There are, however, various state organizations that broadly share the association's outlook and mission, and who communicate and cooperate with the HSLDA.

Ian Slatter, speaking for the HSLDA, could not comment on the specifics of the Borden case, nor with any knowledge on the extent of David Ludwig and Kara Borden's participation in the homeschooling community in Lancaster. He confessed to knowing no more than what he'd read in the newspapers about the case.

"Obviously we accept the view that it was a tragedy," said Slatter, "and not the sort of thing that you would expect to find in the homeschool community."

Slatter explained that it is the parents who have the ultimate responsibility for their children and to the secular laws that govern society. Although he was not apportioning blame, he did say you have to look to what the parents did that might explain a dependent child's behavior.

There is a 2003 commissioned study titled *Homeschooling Grows Up* that surveyed over 7,000 homeschooled graduates. *Homeschooling Grows Up* (compiled by Dr. Brian D. Ray, president of the National Home Education Research Institute) is the largest research survey to date of adults who were home-educated. Over the last decade, researchers, professionals, parents, the media, and many others have asked repeatedly: How do homeschooled students turn out? Can a homeschool graduate get into college or get a job? How do they fit into society? Are they good citizens? Are they happy?

Homeschoolers, the study found, were significantly above average in voting patterns, participation in community groups, and in the ability to find work across all professions. Slatter says the homeschooling environment is a better one, in socialization terms, for the child than the public or private sector. He can say that because in school a child socializes only within their "peer segregated band." That is an artificial environment, says Slatter.

"A homeschooler, on the other hand, will be meeting adults on a regular basis and socialize with other children as part of a homeschool co-op. The HSLDA believes this to be a much closer representation of what life will be like as an adult. So, a homeschooled child will have an advantage in learning to be part of a wider community."

The HSLDA encourages member families to interact with other people in the community to forward the education of their children. The HSLDA suggests teaming up with a co-op to take advantage of group activities and participate in any drama productions, bands and sports leagues.

The association does not dictate to member families how they should homeschool, because, says Slatter, there are "a thousand and one ways to successfully homeschool." But, he adds, the association would be deeply concerned if the parents kept their kids within the four walls of their home and did not make any effort to reach out and interact with other families.

The HSLDA is "Christian-led"—that is, the leadership and the attorneys are practicing Christians. The association does not have a "statement of faith" in its charter. Slatter says the association happily accepts families of all faiths, or atheists, and that is why they do not have a statement of faith.

Ian Slatter says the problems the Bordens and the Ludwigs had with their children in Lititz were family issues, and not endemic to the community of home-schoolers.

SEVENTEEN

A Red Flag

On Wednesday, November 23, a report of a suspected affair between David Ludwig and yet another under-aged girl surfaced on the Internet. John Powers, a webmaster and journalist for the online news magazine www.actionreport.net, wrote that he had received from an anonymous source portions of e-mails from the now-defunct komputerkid16@yahoo.com—David Ludwig's e-mail address.

It appears that while on a Hawaiian vacation in 2004, David Ludwig had begun a relationship with a teenage girl who was affiliated with a church he attended in Kailua. The content of the e-mails seemed to suggest that a sexual relationship had developed between the two.

From reading these e-mails, the media immediately began to suggest that David Ludwig seemed to use his "faith in the same way other men use sports cars—as a hook." It seemed to them that his religion appeared to be "a tool with which he manipulated the young woman in Hawaii."

When the pair returned to their respective homes, an exchange of e-mails between them ensued. In a telling communiqué, the infatuated girl wrote David the following:

I'm also sorry that I let "us" go as far as I did. I guess I just believed that same old lie that somehow this one would be different. As much as it hurts, I never go into something like that anymore thinking it's going to last forever I regret that I became a stumbling block rather than encouraging you the way a sister in Christ should have, but I don't regret spending time with you or anything we did.

Maybe you do, but I don't. I truly had fun and loved [[almost :-)]] every minute of it. I've never dated a guy that cared so much about me before or who actually tried to help me out when I was being a total biotch. Whether lust or love based, God can use you even if you don't mean him to. You were probably my best friend and really meant a lot to me. You really made me think . . . even before our little talk today.

Reading into the words of the young girl, it seems obvious that the two engaged in some sexual activity, and that the girl felt used. She further wrote the following:

I also just thought I'd let you know that I put you on my AIM block list not because I don't like you or don't want to talk to you ever again, but because I do and I think for now I need to just let it go.

I don't really expect you to reply to this or frankly even read the whole thing, but I just wanted to say thanks for

talking to me and I'm sorry for this whole mess. I'm gonna
miss you a lot. . . . but I guess it's for the best.

After all God has a pretty good track record of bein right:)

Detective Sergeant Larry Martin of the county's
MCFU investigated still another incident involving
Ludwig and an underaged girl.

Martin had been called in to work the case at 10
AM the day of the murders while he was at church, approximately two hours after the Bordens had been
shot. He was detailed to Warwick police HQ and while
there, was assisting Detective Kerry Sweigart in the
interview of Kara's sister Katelyn (interviewing of
material witnesses was always performed by two detectives). Three days later, and still on the case, Martin
got orders to follow up on a lead that had been called
in. It required him to make a ninety-minute-long drive
northwest to Juniata County on the other side of the
Susquehanna River. Juniata is a very rural and wooded
county where many suburban dwellers maintain hunting cabins, as did the Ludwigs.

Martin met with a property owner whose parcel of
land adjoined the Ludwigs'. What Martin discovered
was that the neighbor wanted to notify police of an incident that had happened approximately six months before. The neighbor thought it had some bearing on the
then–still-missing teenagers.

In the spring of 2005 the neighbor had received a
call from Mr. Ludwig, who asked him to check their
cabin to see if his son David was there. When the neighbor drove over to the Ludwig cabin, he discovered a
car in the driveway. After knocking on the door, David

emerged bare-chested with a handgun tucked in his waistband. There was a young girl about David's age inside the small cabin. The neighbor told the teenager that his parents were concerned about him and he was to call home immediately.

When the neighbor returned to his cabin, he placed a call to Mr. Ludwig and told him what he'd discovered. Later that day Mr. Ludwig and the girl's father arrived at the cabin and took their kids home. Sergeant Martin and Ed Tobin later learned that the young girl was a reported runaway. Her parents did not file charges with the authorities, notifying them that the incident would be dealt with between the two families. Police, at the time, considered it a closed case.

Detective Ed Tobin would later interview the young girl about that weekend to determine an MO that might be used in the prosecution's case against Ludwig in a trial. Tobin said the girl's family "was reluctant to get involved, they sort of wanted to put the whole incident behind them."

EIGHTEEN

Night Patrols

Among the items of interest taken by the search warrant team when they executed the order on the Ludwig home on West Orange Street in Lititz on November 13 were the hard drives in David's computers. The repositories of data were speculated to contain a wealth of information on the murder suspect, since David Ludwig was known as a computer geek. The information computer forensic Detective Chris Erb gleaned from the hard drives did not disappoint the authorities.

No doubt the most eye-opening item found was an eighteen-minute video downloaded from a camera depicting a home invasion by David and Sam Lohr, who were brandishing firearms while dressed in black. The stealthy intruders in the videos referred to their nocturnal forays as "night patrols."

District Attorney Donald Totaro said he was "shocked at how cold and calculating Ludwig appeared in the video," and how "chilling" it was to watch it. But the DA also must have been secretly pleased by the discovery of it, because he knew how damaging this kind of evidence would be for any attempt by an attorney to mount a credible defense for Ludwig in case it went to trial.

Not only was the video solid evidence of the crime of criminal trespassing, but if also showed David's state of mind. Totaro knew this discovery would prove to be devastating to the defense of David Ludwig. The fact that the hard drives were legally obtained through search warrants would make the evidence bulletproof to any ploy by the defense to have it suppressed.

Sam Lohr had reported to the police at their mobile unit the morning of the murders and says he told them "everything," but since the night patrols had occurred months before, he had completely forgotten about them. When he voluntarily went to the police, he'd brought David's laptop, which he'd been designing a program for. He was not trying to hide anything that would implicate him in any crime.

Lohr's identity as Ludwig's cohort was quickly confirmed on the video by Detective Eric Zimmerman.

For this second interview, Lohr was picked up on November 19. MCFU partner Detective John Schofield of the Lititz Borough PD would assist in the questioning. Zimmerman said that Lohr was obviously frightened during the interview, but very cooperative in giving information.

The planning of the night patrols, not surprisingly, was done via the Internet, specifically Xanga. Forensic computer detective Chris Erb was able to lift the threads from David and Sam's computer hard drives.

Lohr had handled most of the camera work, since he wanted to pursue a career as a filmmaker, and had a flair for drama. Lohr, at 5' 6", was not as tall and muscular or as handsome as David. He was not as popular with the girls, but he seemed to bask in the glow of the charismatic Ludwig, whom he idolized, said Detective Zimmerman. Ludwig was the self-appointed leader, Sam was the follower who admittedly "loved and admired" David.

The pair would meet at Ludwig's house, go into the bunker—the "secured room"—where they would pick out the guns they would carry. Once armed, the pair would pile into a car and drive through the darkened streets of Lititz. Conversations of their plans and David's boasting of how he could easily break into houses without being discovered were caught on video.

In the depicted night patrol, they arrive at the house under the veil of a dark moonless night. Exiting the car, the video shows Ludwig making his way with Lohr up to a private residence on a wooded lot. Both boys speak in low voices to each other to plan an armed forcible entry into the home by climbing up onto the roof and entering through a dormer window. Ludwig and Lohr talk about using their weapons to shoot and kill family members inside the house.

As the pair proceed to execute their plan, an increase in car traffic spooks them and has them aborting their mission. The boys retreat back to their car, get in and drive off.

Detective Chris Erb, the computer forensic detective who'd located the video file on Ludwig's laptop, found it to be "very disturbing," reminding him of the video that Eric Harris and Dylan Klebold had made prior to the Columbine massacre where twelve students and a teacher were mowed down by the deranged pair in a Denver, Colorado, suburb in 1999.

"The way they carried themselves, the clothing they had worn and the weaponry they had carried," Erb said, "was eerily reminiscent of Columbine. And for them to conduct such a patrol on an innocent household was serious stuff. If they had been stopped by police, for, say, a traffic infringement, I am convinced that, since they were armed, a shoot-out would have ensued, and God knows how many people would have been hurt or killed."

Later, on November 21, 2004, Lohr confessed to another night patrol he'd made with David, which detectives had learned about from 16-year-old Alita Stoner, who'd told of the break-in during an interview with police, according to court documents. Alita had been questioned by detectives because of her friendship with Ludwig. This time the target house was the home of John Ambrose, another homeschooler, whom Ludwig considered an adversary.

Lohr admitted he had entered the house through a rear door and let Ludwig and Stoner in through the garage. Lohr claims he had not been carrying a weapon, and had he known David was, he "would have been outta there." Stoner, who was not charged, because she was a cooperating witness, willingly entered the home of the unsuspecting family with David Ludwig. The trio got spooked by a family member stirring, and quickly vacated the home.

District Attorney Totaro said Stoner was ". . . extremely cooperative with police, and without her cooperation, the Commonwealth could not have proceeded against Mr. Lohr on the present charges.

"The family was not aware that anyone unlawfully

entered their home," Totaro said. "Furthermore, in his
first statement to police, Mr. Lohr made no reference to
entering the house. The police did not become aware of
the home invasion until Ms. Stoner was interviewed and
provided that information. When confronted with the
statement of Alita Stoner, Mr. Lohr admitted to unlawfully entering the home, but he was not carrying a gun.

"Given the adult age of Mr. Lohr," Totaro related,
"and the violent nature of his conduct (as established
by the criminal complaint and affidavit), it was agreed
that Alita Stoner would not be referred to juvenile court
in exchange for her cooperation against Mr. Lohr." A
court date was scheduled for March 29.

Once David met Kara, the break-ins had continued, but now his attention was focused on the home
on Royal Drive in Warwick Township.

Lohr told Zimmerman and Schofield of one such
early-morning intrusion where the two climbed up on
the roof of the house. Lohr remained on the roof while
David opened the window to Kara's bedroom and
slipped inside. According to Lohr, David engaged in
sexual activity with Kara while her parents slept down
the hall. Lohr bided his time as a faithful lookout on
the roof. Lohr also said that David had told him that he
had broken into the Borden residence at 2 AM, just a
few weeks before the murders.

Contrary to what appeared in the newspapers, Lohr
never indicated, to David or the police, any desire to
have sex with Kara's older sister Katelyn, though, explained Lohr, David did say in the video that Sam
should "hook up" with her.

"I never had any interest in Katelyn," Lohr told the
author.

Zimmerman, through his interviews with Lohr, was convinced that Sam was a "non-aggressive individual" and had only followed his buddy on the night patrols for want of some excitement. Ludwig, however, was a different story. He had made it clear to Lohr that he didn't want to get caught by Kara's parents on the late-night trysting forays, and that was why he always carried guns that he was ready to use if necessary.

The Warwick detectives were sure after learning about the night patrols that the murders of the Bordens could have happened at any time. David's stealth and the fact that he was never found out in the break-ins accounted for a few extra months of life for Michael and Cathryn Borden.

Brian Lohr said the incidents involving his son and their repercussions were "a sad subject for us [the Lohr family,] and caused a lot of turmoil.

"We raised our kids," Mr. Lohr said, "to care for people, and unfortunately some people took advantage of that scenario and caused a lot of trouble in a lot of different ways."

Mr. Lohr echoed a common sentiment in the community when talking about his son's involvement in the case by noting his reluctance to speak to the media, saying: "We don't hold the media in high regard."

A few months later, during a brief hearing before Lancaster County Judge David L. Ashworth, Samuel Lohr pleaded guilty to criminal trespass and two counts of illegal firearms possession. At that time there was no agreement on a sentence between Assistant District Attorney K. Kenneth Brown and Lohr's attorney, Janice

Longer. Lohr and Longer only spoke in response to questions from Ashworth.

Lohr, however, did speak with Mrs. Ambrose, who had approached him after the sentencing. She told him that if she had known that they had entered her house, and the murders hadn't happened, she would have just laughed it off.

"It was messed up," Lohr said. "First off, we did not break in, the house was unlocked. The family were friends and we were welcome there anytime—night or day. I was not carrying a gun, and I didn't know if David was or was not. However, in the eyes of the police—I am guilty."

District Attorney Totaro said that, despite reluctance from the trespass victims (who spoke on Lohr's behalf at his sentencing), Lohr entered "open guilty pleas to one count of criminal trespass and firearms not to be carried without a license. The firearms charge was based on his possession of firearms as seen on the 'night patrol' video."

Lohr later said that when he and David carried guns, his was never loaded. He said that carrying them was "so stupid," and he trembled at the thought now that had they been seen, they could easily have been shot. But at the time, they'd thought it was "so cool."

Lohr doesn't think his criminal acts were a result of peer pressure.

"I didn't really have any friends at the time but David, and that's what he was doing. I had nobody else to hang out with, so I said all right. It was the dumbest thing I ever did."

Samuel Lohr would eventually get a sentence of 7 years' probation. According to DA Don Totaro, Lohr's history of sexual abuse played no factor in the charging or prosecution decision. However, his defense attorney did inform Judge Ashworth, prior to sentencing, of the abuse.

"Whether the judge took that into consideration," said Totaro, "would only be speculation on my part."

Janice Longer, Sam's criminal defense attorney, called Sam Lohr "the boy next door."

Longer, a criminal defense practitioner for the last twelve years in Lancaster County, said that Sam was very intelligent, polite and well-meaning. Longer had filed a sentencing memorandum for her client stating that Sam was cooperating with the court, that he had been a victim in another case [the Neidermyer sex abuse case] and had a "number of other mitigating circumstances" that she hoped the court would take into consideration. But she thought there were other more important factors that helped him more.

"It was so out of character for Sam to knowingly commit a crime," Longer said. "The fact that he had no prior record spoke for itself. I was so impressed with his family, their friends and the people from his church. He is an intelligent, talented man. I remember thinking after meeting him for the first time, when the only things I knew about him was what I read in the newspaper, was that the impression I was left with was that this was the kind of boy I'd like my daughter to date."

NINETEEN

The Prosecution

Donald Totaro chose his profession well. He is smart, thoughtful, detail-oriented, well-spoken, ambitious and clean-cut. Lancaster County's criminal defense attorneys have a healthy respect for the dogged DA. Although they may be reluctant to express flattering opinions of their courtroom counterpart, they do give the man his due—he is a worthy opponent in the legal trenches.

A graduate of Northeastern University and American University Washington College of Law, who spent twenty years as an assistant prosecutor in Lancaster County, Totaro has served the last eight years as DA. Totaro has run a tight ship. He restructured the office so that all prosecutors and county detectives are full-time employees and he also left his mark on the county criminal court system by wiping out the backlog of cases, and eliminating plea bargains in homicides, gun felonies and drug cases. His reputation would now be on the line in the county's most famous case to date.

It appeared that the DA was on a mission in the Bordens' murder case. Totaro's law-and-order fervor was evident from the beginning; he spared no quarter to the young defendant and would doggedly prosecute him to the full extent of the law over the next eight months.

Totaro knew he had a strong case against David Ludwig, but he tries to suppress a smile when asked if he thought it was a slam-dunk. It seems the legal cliché is not in his professional vocabulary. The fact that the Bordens' murder case was personally handled by him—only the second in his eight-year tenure as district attorney—and not handed over to one of his seventy able and trial-tested assistant district attorneys was indicative of that. Totaro wanted to make sure that "no stone was left unturned" in the high-profile case.

The national media was watching, and if the DA ever forgot it, all he had to do was look out the window of his office on the fifth floor of the county courthouse in downtown Lancaster to see the line of TV trucks with their satellite dishes on North Duke Street. There were also the journalists' requests for interviews piled on his desk to remind him of the scrutiny the case was under.

The 43-year-old lawyer denies that he was personally handling this one because of his love of cameras, something that had been suggested by more than a few of his critics. Totaro was planning to step down after his present stint as DA and move up to a judgeship (also an elective office); it was just, he claims, that there was no way he was "letting this one get away." No way was his office going to botch this very public prosecution of David Ludwig.

Totaro was at the crime scene early that Sunday morning, November 13, 2005, and huddling with his detectives and the other MCFU investigators. He worked closely with Warwick Chief Richard Garipoli and had his small army of ADAs working overtime.

Things unfolded quickly. The day of the murders, the DA was already aware of the "incident" in Juniata County at the Ludwig family hunting cabin with the underaged female. By the time the fugitives were returned to Pennsylvania from Indiana on Wednesday, November 16, the DA had his ducks lined up. From telephone conversations and reports faxed to them by the Indiana State Police, Totaro and lead detectives Geesey and Tobin were pretty sure the kidnapping charges against Ludwig would have to be dropped.

At Victim/Witness Services on the sixth floor of the courthouse—where Kara had been interviewed with attorney Robert Beyer in attendance—what Totaro's office had to do next was clear: dig further into Kara's possible complicity in the murders of her parents. Totaro and his team of investigators would spend the best part of the next four weeks investigating that angle, and the conclusion they would come to would determine the case strategy.

One thing Totaro knew was that first-degree homicide charges would be filed against David Ludwig. The DA was convinced that the murders were "intentional, deliberate and premeditated on his part."

According to Pennsylvania law, premeditation can be formed in a fraction of a second. It didn't matter, says Totaro, if Ludwig's intent when he armed himself prior to leaving his home on that fateful day was only for his protection.

"As he [Ludwig] was sitting in that house," Totaro said, "after being told by Mr. Borden to go home and tell his parents what had happened, according to both Kara and sister Katelyn, he didn't talk, and just stared into space for five to ten minutes before he was shown to the door and started firing. That is sufficient proof to show his intent and prove first-degree murder."

According to Totaro, Kara had said her father had confronted Ludwig at the door, saw he had guns and told him to leave them outside before he entered the house. Obviously, Mr. Borden was unaware that the boy was carrying a concealed weapon, and Kara had said as much as well, said the DA.

For the next two weeks the prosecution team and investigators met on a daily basis, first at Warwick police HQ then at the DA's office, and reviewed the status of the investigation and what had been done and what had to be done. The focus, since it was clear they had a strong case of first-degree homicide against Ludwig, was then to determine what Kara's involvement was in bringing about the killing of her parents, and if there was sufficient evidence under Pennsylvania law to charge her with murder or any other offenses as an accomplice or as a conspirator. If she was determined to be culpable in the murder of her parents, Totaro personally believed she should be charged; but they would not file any charges that they could not ultimately prove, based upon personal disgust for her conduct.

Totaro says Kara Borden's age was never a factor in deciding whether to charge her. He had no hesitation in prosecuting minors for crimes as adults. He had done it before.

In the early 1990s as an ADA he had prosecuted another 14-year-old. That time it was a boy who, in attempting to shoot another boy in a Lancaster City playground, missed and hit a young girl, who died at the scene. The youthful offender was tried for murder and was convicted.

According to Totaro, in Pennsylvania juvenile murder cases, the defense has the burden of trying to send the case back to Juvenile Court. They have to successfully argue that the youth can be treated and rehabilitated as a juvenile. In the Borden case Totaro was prepared to bring Kara to trial as an adult too. It would come down to the facts of the law.

A lot of people involved in the investigation were troubled by the fact that Kara had known David was coming over to the house with guns, and that she'd never warned her parents, even though it appears Mr. Ludwig figured it out for himself when he saw David carrying the blanket containing the firearms. Also the fact that she'd gotten into the car with David of her own volition after she'd seen him shoot her father in the back of the head—she had fled the room prior to the shooting of her mother—and then later said she wanted to start a new life together with Ludwig bothered many, including Totaro, but did not hold sway over whether charges should be brought.

Some 170 people were interviewed in the effort to determine her complicity. The prosecutors had as evidence ten computers, which included desktops, laptops and PDAs that were scoured for information that might have shed light on this aspect of the case. Weeks were spent to find every contact's name, text message, or instant message that existed on the computers. There was also the information obtained from MySpace and Xanga that was pored over, as well as the pair's cell phone text messages. It was slow, tedious work, especially since most of the time all the investigators had was a screen name. Everybody at David's job at Circuit City, the pair's homeshooling networks, friends and neighborhood canvassing contacts were interviewed.

Totaro knew that if they did charge Kara with complicity, they probably would lose the cooperation of the Borden family, but Donald Totaro believed they could prove the case against David Ludwig without their help or Kara's. The defendant's own statements and the testimony of eyewitnesses Katelyn and David Borden would be enough. The investigation generated over 2,000 pages of evidentiary information.

Throughout, the public focus never strayed far from Kara's involvement and how it should be dealt with by the district attorney. The big difference for the prosecution team was that they could not be held hostage by emotion, despite what each member of the prosecution team may have felt.

Ultimately, the prosecutors could not find that Kara Borden had encouraged, aided, abetted, conspired or agreed in any way for David Ludwig to come over to the Borden home and cause harm to her parents. Totaro said, "We just couldn't do it; we could find no evidence of any kind that could prove her complicity."

Totaro's office was inundated with phone calls, mail and e-mail by people who were generally repulsed by Kara's conduct and wanted her charged accordingly.

"That's why we have judges," says the district attorney. "When DAs make judgments solely on what the public wants to see happen, you always have a judge in place who, at some point in time, is going to say, 'You haven't met the burden of proof.'"

The judge, of course, is a little more removed than a prosecutor from the pressure of public opinion, and if he fails, there is always the appellate court, who is going to look at cases in a vacuum.

Not only did the prosecution look carefully at Pennsylvania law, but also at other states' laws, and at federal statutes as well. In dealing with the national media, many of their legal experts asked about charging Kara Borden with accessory after the fact:

> *Whoever, knowing that an offense has been committed, receives, relieves, comforts or assists the offender in order to hinder or prevent his apprehension, trial or punishment, is an accessory after the fact; one who knowing a felony to have been committed by another, receives, relieves, comforts, or assists the felon in order to hinder the felon's apprehension, trial, or punishment. U.S.C. 18.*

In Pennsylvania there is no accessory after the fact, it having been abolished from the state's statute years ago (twenty states still have it on the books).

One aspect of the case that was looked at very closely was who had disposed of the two personal phones when the couple fled Lititz. If they could prove that Kara had thrown one or both cell phones out of the car on the way out of town to avoid apprehension, the prosecution might have grounds for charging her. But in David Ludwig's statement, he was clear that it had been him, and only him, who had disposed of the cell phones.

The prosecution also examined a number of cases decided by the Pennsylvania appellate courts for guidance. In *Commonwealth* v. *Fields*, where the facts disclosed that a person had arrived at a crime scene with the killer, was present during the killing and even asked the victim provocative questions, the Pennsylvania Supreme Court held that foreknowledge that a crime may be committed and even presence at the scene does not render a person an accomplice.

In *Commonwealth* v. *Richey*, where two wives who knew beforehand that a robbery had been planned, had witnessed the crime and received a share of the proceeds; the Pennsylvania Superior Court held that they were not accomplices because they'd lacked the requisite intent.

In *Commonwealth* v. *Murphy*, the Pennsylvania Supreme Court held that a defendant cannot be an accomplice simply based on evidence that he knew about the crime or was present at the crime scene; there must be some additional evidence that the defendant had intended to aid in the commission of the underlying crime and then did or attempted to do so. As the court stated, mere association with the perpetrators, mere presence at the scene, or mere knowledge of the crime is insufficient to establish that the person was part of an agreement to commit the crime.

In *Commonwealth* v. *Manchas*, the Pennsylvania Superior Court reviewed a number of prior cases holding that, to be an accomplice, one must be an active partner in the intent to commit the crime; an accomplice must have done something to participate in the venture; a showing of mere presence at the scene of a crime is insufficient to support a conviction; even presence at the scene of a crime in the company of its perpetrator has been held to be insufficient to sustain a conviction.

The prosecution also looked at similar cases that were won, only to have been reversed on appeal. One case in 1992 was a good indicator of what the Lancaster DA might run into.

In the case—*Commonwealth* v. *Pestinikas*—the Superior Court actually upheld the third-degree murder conviction against the defendant because evidence showed that death had been caused by the defendants' failure to provide food and medical care for which they had previously agreed by oral contract to provide to the victim. In that case, the Superior Court held that there are four situations where failure to act may constitute breach of a legal duty warranting criminal charges. They are: 1) where a statute imposes a duty of care for another; 2) where one stands in a certain status relationship to another; 3) where one has assumed a contractual duty to care for another; or 4) where one has voluntarily assumed the care of another and so secluded the helpless person as to prevent others from rendering aid.

In *Pestinikas*, the court noted that while the failure to provide food and medicine to an elderly person cannot be the basis for a homicide prosecution against a stranger who learns of that person's condition and fails to act, failure to provide such food or medicine by someone who agreed to do so is sufficient to support a homicide charge. Although the court upheld the conviction in *Pestinikas* under those facts, the Superior Court used language to distinguish these specific legal duties to act from "merely a moral duty to act." In the Borden case, the actions of Kara did not fall within any of the four legal duties to act. There was no statute in Pennsylvania that imposes on a child the duty of care for their parents. Kara did not stand in a certain status relationship with her parents that warranted a duty of care (the reverse is true: this duty exists on the part of a parent, guardian or caregiver to a child). There was no contractual relationship between Kara and her parents. Furthermore, Kara did not voluntarily assume the care of her parents or seclude them.

Totaro explained that a legal obligation to warn in the reverse (parent to child) is unambiguous because parents/guardians have a legal obligation to care for a child, but legal obligation of a child to parent was another story.

The appellate courts have made very clear that under the facts known in the Borden murders, the DA's office would not be legally justified in charging Kara Borden. Furthermore, if they did so, any possible conviction would have been reversed on appeal before these very same courts.

The high court made it very clear in its instruction to a jury about accomplices:

You may find that the defendant is an accomplice of another if the following two elements are proved beyond a reasonable doubt. One, the defendant had the intent of promoting or facilitating the commission of the offense. Two, the defendant solicits, commands, encourages, requests the other person to commit it or aids, agrees to aid, or attempts to aid the other person in planning or committing it.

Early in the proceedings Totaro related that the defense counsel had floated the prospect that their client might implicate Kara if it would help his case. Totaro was all ears.

"Give me what you have," Totaro wrote in e-mails to defense counsel, but he was quick to add he would cut Ludwig no deals. The defense then made it quite clear that if their client agreed to tell the DA about Kara's complicity, he would have to get a deal.

Totaro rationalized his unwillingness to cut a deal by saying he would not compromise with a man "who put two bullets through the heads of two innocent victims" and then tried to get a deal from the prosecution by "getting at their daughter."

"Even if we were, in my mind, foolish enough to make a deal with Ludwig to go after Kara, would a jury ever believe Ludwig?" Totaro had ruminated. In two previous statements Ludwig had never implicated Kara, and basically absolved her of any guilt in the deaths of her parents.

"And now he sits facing the death penalty," Totaro said, "and suddenly changes what he had said and make[s] her complicit in exchange for a deal?" Totaro said that the deal would have to be made known to a jury in any trial of Kara, adding, "I don't think any juror would find him credible. That would have meant that she would have walked and Ludwig has his deal."

The prosecution would also have demanded corroboration in the form of a letter, e-mail or text message if they were to deal. There was no such evidence.

"At the end of the day," related the DA, "what we were dealing with here was very questionable moral conduct on her part as opposed to conduct that is chargeable under the law."

Upon completion of their investigation of Kara's conduct, Totaro was purposeful in letting the Borden family know that the prosecution had found no evidence pointing to Kara as a co-conspirator or an abettor in the murders.

Once Kara was cleared of any wrongdoing, Totaro added the firearms and the statutory sexual assault charges to the first-degree murder(s) charges. These new charges could only be proved with Kara's help and testimony if the case went to trial. Under Pennsylvania law it is called the *Corpus delicti* rule. Before you can admit someone's confession, you have to have independent evidence that a crime occurred. The reasoning for the Corpus delicti (literally the "body of crime") rule being that the state didn't want to convict a person based on a false confession. Kara's testimony, the Corpus delicti, would have backed David Ludwig's statements regarding the statutory rape and weapons offenses.

Specifically, Kara had to be ready to admit in front of an open courtroom—if it went to trial—that she and David had engaged in sexual intercourse several times between September 7, 2005, and November 13, 2005. It would be a difficult confession to make for any teenage girl in front of family, friends and strangers, but it would have to be done. She said she would do it.

By December 16, the decision had been made that the prosecution would be going after David Ludwig as the sole perpetrator in the murders of Michael and

Cathryn Borden, with Kara Borden as a witness for the prosecution.

The surviving Borden family members "felt fairly strongly that they would do nothing to impede the prosecution," said DA Totaro, but if there was any way to resolve the case without putting Kara, Katelyn or David on the stand, they wanted that avenue pursued.

According to Totaro, the family wasn't naïve about what would probably happen if Kara took the stand. They knew the defense counsel would surely question her conduct in the incident and were aware of what that would do to her. The reliving of the horrible events of November 13, 2005, by siblings Katelyn and David would have been a nightmare. Despite that, the Borden family was determined that David Ludwig be held accountable for murdering the family patriarch and matriarch, and that justice was done.

Early on, defense counsel had been in touch with Totaro's office about removing the death penalty from the table. They believed there was a distinct possibility that their client would plead guilty to first-degree murder for life in prison. Totaro told them, nevertheless, that he would be filing notice with the courts that he would seek death.

In Pennsylvania a prosecutor has to file notice of his intent to seek a death penalty by the date of the arraignment or it couldn't be filed at all. What that meant was that if the defendant reneged on the deal to plead guilty, the prosecution couldn't go back and request death, since they hadn't initially filed notice. Totaro was not going to allow that to happen.

According to the DA, there were three "aggravators" that would justify pursuing the death penalty:

Number One: The defendant had committed a murder while in perpetration of a felony.

Number Two: In the commission of the offense the defendant had knowingly created a grave risk of death to another person or persons—Kara, Katelyn and David Borden—in addition to the victim(s), Michael and Cathryn Borden.

Number Three: The defendant had been convicted of another murder committed in any jurisdiction and committed either before or at the time of the offense at issue—the shooting death of Michael Borden that preceded the shooting death of Cathryn Borden.

The district attorney gave strong consideration to the wishes of victims' families when it came to the penalty phase of the case, hence the Borden family was very much involved in deciding whether David Ludwig would pay for his crimes with his life. Due to the wide dispersal of the family across the country, Pamela Grosh, director of the Victim/Witness Services—part of the DA's office—was the liaison to them. Several conference calls between the prosecution team and the Borden family would help to decide if the defense counsel would be able to negotiate the death penalty off the table. The one condition that Totaro required of any decision by the family was that it be unanimous.

In the first conference call, DA Totaro basically laid out the law as it applied in the Keystone State. He addressed the different options in the prosecution of the accused, aggravating circumstances, what would have to be proved, and what all witnesses would have to go through in the event of a trial in order to get a conviction and then get to the penalty phase.

In Pennsylvania the decision on punishment is a separate hearing from the trial. It only happens when a jury comes back with a first-degree murder conviction. Anything less—that is, a conviction on second degree, third degree or manslaughter, and the penalty phase is dispensed with, since sentencing is up to the judges' discretion.

Totaro foresaw that defense counsel would be arguing for a lesser charge, insisting that David Ludwig had brought the guns over for protection and had used one to kill the Bordens in the heat of passion and then, during the discussion with Mr. Borden, had lost control and proceeded to shoot the couple.

The jury had the option of effecting a compromise. That is, the prosecution would be arguing first-degree murder, the defense manslaughter and the jury could come back with a third-degree conviction (voluntary or involuntary manslaughter are unjustified killings without malice that carry probation to 10 years; third-degree murder, a catch-all charge, carries 20–40 years in prison; second-degree murder is a felony murder where the perpetrator kills without intent, but in the commission of a crime such as armed robbery, and carries life with no parole).

The defense, of course, would put up some mitigators identified by the Pennsylvania state legislature as potentially affecting sentencing. There was David Ludwig's young age and his lack of a prior record for the jury to take into consideration in mitigating against the death penalty.

The district attorney knew he would have to educate the jury during any trial that the laws that relate to the death penalty are understood and that the aggravating circumstances existed and far outweighed the mitigating circumstances, and the death penalty was the proper sentence.

The prosecution would have to prove to all twelve jurors that death was the correct sentence; the defense would just have to convince one juror of the mitigators and it would be life in prison without the possibility of parole.

What transpired over the next few months was a seemingly endless string of motions by the defense counsel, and counter-motions by the prosecution regarding the disposition of the case. DA Totaro explained the delays:

> "Based upon my twenty years as a prosecutor I can tell you that it usually takes about one year from date of arrest until final disposition in a homicide case. This case was no different, and I do not believe there were unusual delays. Despite early indications that Ludwig might enter a guilty plea to first-degree murder, it was essential that the Commonwealth and defense counsel proceed and prepare as if the case was going to trial. There were thousands of pages of reports and documents that had to be reviewed by the Commonwealth and submitted to defense as part of the discovery process. The defense needed sufficient time to examine those documents, file motions and explore mental health defense options. Any shortcuts could have resulted in Ludwig obtaining new counsel after

his guilty plea and filing a motion demanding a new trial by alleging his trial counsel was ineffective in representing him. That possibility was something the defense attorneys and I wanted to avoid at all costs."

As the month of May approached and the prosecution and defense were nearing the suppression of evidence hearings and a June 16 trial, Totaro learned from family contact person Pam Grosh that the Borden family was mostly leaning toward life without the possibility of parole in lieu of death.

In the final conference call it was unanimous: life without parole. The Borden family felt very strongly that if Kara, Katelyn and David didn't have to testify, that that was the route they wanted to take.

Totaro took this back to the defense counsel, who in turn presented it to the client, and ultimately he agreed.

TWENTY

The Defense

Merrill Spahn, a criminal defense attorney, and his law partner, Sam Encarnacion, maintain a suite of offices in a fashionable brownstone directly across the street from the Lancaster County Courthouse on East Orange Street in downtown Lancaster.

Besides criminal law, he and his partner pursue civil litigation and immigration cases, but after speaking with the attorney briefly, one quickly learns where his passion in law lies—litigating capital punishment cases.

A bear of a man, Spahn looks more like a football coach than a public defender tilting at the windmills of pro–death penalty public sentiment in the historically conservative county. He appears to be a man who relishes the good fight. His job would be a challenging one from the beginning in the ides of November 2005.

Just two days after the murder of the Borden couple, when the fleeing young lovers were captured in Indiana, Spahn knew he would be representing David Ludwig.

Spahn has been practicing law since 1992, the bulk of it working as a public defender in Lancaster County.

Spahn was, and is, the deputy chief of the Public Defender's Office throughout the legal ordeal of the Borden homicides case.

James Gratton, another public defender, was paired with Spahn to handle David Ludwig's case from the outset when the accused was brought back from Indiana. Although both men worked on all aspects of the case jointly, Gratton's primary duty would be Ludwig's guilt phase; Spahn's was to be the penalty phase, or the all-important, unresolved life-and-death issue of the sensational case.

Merrill Spahn said that there was no lobbying on his or Gratton's part to get the case. He wrote:

> *The PDs* [Public Defenders] *office takes all death penalty homicides in Lancaster Co. unless a conflict of interest exists. I am the deputy chief public defender there.*
>
> *There are 7 lawyers within that office that do death penalty work. The chief pd* [Public Defender] *makes all case assignments. I have done more mitigation work than anyone in that office. I am routinely assigned to some of the most serious homicide case. No, there was nothing unusual about our appointment nor was there any lobbying to get the appointment.*

In the Commonwealth, anyone who is incarcerated is provided with a public defender regardless of income or wealth. Mr. Ludwig had a six-figure job and owned a home in Lititz, certainly indicating he could afford a private, high-profile lawyer to handle his son's case.

Because of Supreme Court constraints and what has

to be done legally in a capital case—the costs of two lawyers, expert witnesses, private investigators—Spahn estimated that the legal bill would have been in excess of $100,000, a sum he was not sure Mr. Ludwig could afford. Also, lawyers handling capital cases have to be certified by the state to represent the felon; Spahn is so certified.

Part of the reason Merrill Spahn was selected was District Attorney Don Totaro's policy of seeking the death penalty in such cases.

"For whatever reason," said Spahn somewhat acerbically, "the district attorney [Totaro] in Lancaster County for the last eight years has decided that any time they believe an aggravating circumstance exists they will invoke and request *the penalty* [death]. A lot of DAs in other municipalities don't adopt that rationale."

Since the mid-1990s Spahn has represented approximately 75 percent of the capital punishment cases in Lancaster County, meaning that at any given time he usually has two life-or-death cases before the bench.

The Lancaster County Public Defender's Office was mandated by the United States Supreme Court to appoint two PDs to handle the potential capital case, hence Gratton for the guilt phase and Spahn for the penalty phase. In addition there would have to be an investigator for the front end of the case, for the guilt phase, and for the back end, or the penalty phase, to ferret out potential witnesses.

If there was any intent on the part of the two defense attorneys to garner attention for themselves, as some suspected, they could have done so during their representation of David Ludwig, claimed Spahn. The two defense attorneys turned down offers from all three network morning shows, several cable outlets, and multiple network news magazine shows. They did so, said Spahn, ". . . because publicity would not have benefited our client."

Spahn was also honoring the Ludwig family wishes of privacy. Consequently he has not commented on the David Ludwig case beyond the obligatory short statements to the press—until now.

Capital punishment was officially established in Pennsylvania in 1913 and until 1962, there were a total of 350 persons executed in the electric chair, two of whom were women. But the death penalty in the Commonwealth was declared unconstitutional in January 1971. In 1974, the legislature resurrected the law with amendments passed over the veto of Governor Milton Shapp. In a U.S. Supreme Court decision in *Gregg* v. *Georgia*, the court decided that the 1974 version of the death penalty was too narrowly limited in the circumstances that the jury may consider mitigating when making its decision on capital punishment.

The state legislature, with a finger firmly on the pulse of the electorate, drafted a new version. It was enacted in September 1978, again over the veto of Governor Shapp. This law, which remains in effect today, has been upheld by the U.S. Supreme Court.

On November 29, 1990, Governor Robert P. Casey signed legislation changing Pennsylvania's method of execution from electrocution to lethal injection. The electric chair and all of its associated equipment were removed from the capital punishment complex at SCI Rockview in December 1990 and subsequently turned over to the Pennsylvania Historical and Museum Commission.

On May 2, 1995, Keith Zettlemoyer became the first person executed by lethal injection in Pennsylvania. Since that date, one additional man has been executed by lethal injection. Both had given up their right of appeal.

The Third Circuit Court of Appeals (the Superior Court of Pennsylvania—the appellate court) is comprised of fifteen judges, who usually sit in panels of three to preside over appeals. They are not separated by region, but hear cases at different locations throughout the state. This court has a reputation of being liberal and anti–death penalty, showing a propensity for overturning death sentences.

Still, there are four condemned inmates—Orlando Baez, Tedor Davido, Francis Harris, Landon D. May—from Lancaster County who are to pay the ultimate penalty for their crimes. The four now sit on death row in the remote, austere and high-tech SCI Greene prison in Waynesburg, south of Pittsburgh. The maximum security prison opened in November 1993 as a close-security institution for men, and it houses most of the state's capital case inmates.

One outsider, journalist Cynthia Blumenthal, on a recent visit to Pennsylvania's death row, called the prison "sterile and frightening," noting the prison felt like "a high tech biotechnology lab or perhaps a brand new conference center where no one had had time to do any landscaping." She found its "pristine spotlessness and modernity" more unsetting than the old state prison where she volunteers, partly because it seemed "devoid of any sign of humanity or life." She also noted that the space for visitors to talk to inmates was "only slightly larger than a phone booth, with a stool, and a glass partition."

Realistically, defense attorney Spahn, at this point, does not think a death penalty will ever be carried out in the Commonwealth of Pennsylvania again. He believes the state will go the route of what neighboring New Jersey did recently in December 2007 and consign the contentious issue to the history books, ridding the state of the onerous task of putting to death inmates convicted of murder. But as an advocate for the condemned, he cannot count on that supposition. Politics being what they are, chances cannot be taken with a person's life, especially with a district attorney who would press for the death penalty with a predictable predatory vigor.

Still the question remains, why was the defense counsel so eager to see the death penalty removed from the table early on in David Ludwig's case, at the cost of accepting life without parole for their teenaged client? Since the sentence of death is highly unlikely to be carried out, why not risk pleading your case in front of a jury and hope for a less serious conviction or even an innocent finding? Spahn smiles and says it is a naïve way of thinking.

The reality is there is a night-and-day difference between serving a sentence on death row as opposed to serving life without parole. Although a prisoner serving the life sentence is never getting out like a death row inmate, his existence as a lifer is far more humane than his counterpart in the condemned one's world.

In Pennsylvania the death penalty means solitary confinement for the inmates. They are locked up twenty-three-and-a-half hours a day with a half hour of exercise allowed in an area the size of a dog pen. Death row inmates are allowed no visitations except for ministerial or legal representation visits. Serving a life sentence, conversely, the inmate is in the general population, where he can pursue educational opportunities, receive visitors and take advantage of recreational and exercise time. Lifers can also pursue employment in a prison setting and earn money.

It is very much a quality-of-life issue, and there are "qualitative differences" between the two sentences.

The other thing that goes into the decision in this regard is "the cross benefit analysis." In any criminal case, in considering a plea offer, a defendant must assess the offer advanced by the prosecution against the likelihood of a better result at trial. If you can't reasonably achieve a result at trial better than the offer on the table, then it makes no sense to try the case, regardless of the severity of the offer.

Spahn says the decision to make a deal was the hardest he had ever been involved in with a client and his family. However, it was unanimous, and the defense team had absolutely no doubt that the legal decision was fundamentally solid under all of the circumstances that the case presented.

Defense counsel acknowledges that there is a strategic advantage in seeking the death penalty that has nothing to do with politics, but everything to do with winning and losing cases. It is twofold.

One: Statistically, studies have shown that capital juries—juries that have been certified for death cases—are more apt to convict on the front end of the trial, the guilt phase.

Two: There is a school of thought in law that if you do not use the death penalty option consistently, then the prosecution runs the risk of having it brought up by the defense in the event their client is thus charged. Specifically that means if a defendant is charged with a capital crime, the defense can challenge on *due process* grounds, claiming the death penalty is being used discriminately, i.e., another defendant charged with the same crime did not face death. The prosecution is always concerned with that challenge, and with good reason, since Ludwig's defense team would have surely raised it had they gone to trial.

It was common knowledge that in Indiana, David Ludwig had made two statements to the police, and in both, he'd been very forthcoming with the officers and very admitting of his conduct; on some level that had not changed. The fact that David made admissions squared with what people close to him would have expected, claimed Merrill Spahn.

"Externally," says Spahn, "David was a wonderful kid, a wonderful student and had maintained a job all the while and had no criminal record. Frankly, as I had stated before publicly, he did have some psychological issues under the surface that led to the action here."

As part of their due diligence, there was an extensive psychological work-up on David. Part of that would have been to consider insanity, diminished capacity or any mental illness that would rise to a level of defense in the Commonwealth of Pennsylvania.

Counsel retained Jerome I. Gottlieb, MD, and Gerald Cooke, PhD, to conduct forensic neuropsychiatric and neuropsychological evaluations of their client.

Part of that evaluation was a CT scan of the defendant at the Lancaster General Hospital on March 30, 2006.

According to Spahn, the findings were most definitely mitigating factors, and would have been brought to the attention of a jury.

It has been the position of DA Totaro that in these types of situations, the prosecution will not formally extend the option of removing the death penalty in lieu of a deal. Totaro has always expected defense counsel to make the first move and come to him and ask, "Is this possible?" The DA would make his own determination, then take it to the victims' family and clear it with them. There would be many initial discussions between the court adversaries before a deal was struck.

Pennsylvania is one of just a handful of states where if a convicted felon gets life, the felon *does life*. The only way out of a life sentence is a commutation by the governor after review by the pardons board. In the recent history of Pennsylvania judicial pardons, there has just been one, a terminally ill female inmate who died shortly after her release.

The Ludwig case had been extremely frustrating for Merrill Spahn. From all external perspectives, one would never have expected that David Ludwig was capable of such horrible crimes. Spahn believes David knows psychologically what led him to commit the murders, but it has not lessened the tragedy of it all for him or his family. Making a horrible choice out of desperation will haunt him the rest of his life.

TWENTY-ONE

Covering Their Asses

Susan Moyer, as one courtroom insider put it, is in the district attorney's office for one reason and that is, "to cover the DA's ass." It's a crude way to put it, but it is basically true. Moyer is chief of the Appeals Unit for the Lancaster County District Attorney and does her best to make sure the legal staff dot all their *i*'s and cross all their *t*'s so the office is not subject to the higher courts overturning their convictions—the kind of thing that doesn't get a DA re-elected.

As an assistant district attorney since 1991, Moyer has seen first-hand the worst of human nature. Nothing surprises her anymore. Within the last three years not only has she worked on the David Ludwig case, but also on the Jesse Dee Wise multiple homicide case (in a fit of psychotic rage, Wise executed six family members) and the incomprehensible murders of five Amish schoolchildren in 2006 by sex-obsessed pedophile Charles Carl Roberts IV. Justice, of course, is always a case-by-case determination.

The David Ludwig case was rare for the fact that it was the only one in Susan Moyer's memory where a homicide conviction wasn't challenged by the defense counsel in a higher court. According to Moyer, there were many reasons for that. She speculates that Ludwig's willingness to shoulder the blame and not appeal might make him a more attractive candidate for a pardon from the governor years down the road.

"Many times with a criminal prosecution," Moyer said, "justice doesn't necessarily mean what the public thinks. We [the DA's office] proceed with a case in a manner that is legally correct right down the line. That means protecting the defendants' rights too, as well as the victims' and those of the people of the Commonwealth. It doesn't serve us well if we run ahead with a prosecution and we incorrectly approve a search warrant, because that will come back to haunt you. Evidence like that will get suppressed. One of the big ways that worked with me in the Ludwig case was with Kara Borden."

Moyer says one of the first tasks her office had to tackle was getting a guardian assigned to Kara by the court to make sure her rights were protected when she was still in Indiana and when she was returned to Pennsylvania. They could have simply picked her up and, as Moyer says, "let our detectives go at her." But Moyer knew that any statements would not have held up to the higher court's scrutiny.

In the *People* v. *David Ludwig*, it was the crime that was *not* prosecuted that garnered all the attention and the legal interest in a case that drew national attention: that is, Kara's culpability in the murder of her parents.

Moyer was the researcher who looked into all possibilities as to whether they could charge Kara in the deaths of her parents. She had to be careful, like her boss, the DA, about keeping it from becoming an emotional case against Kara as opposed to a case based solely on the law.

Even though Kara didn't tell her father that David was coming over with guns that fateful day, the fact that David was asked to leave the guns outside, and complied, made Kara feel better, perhaps sensing that her parents were in no danger. In her defense, much could be made of the fact that she'd never seen David personally in possession of firearms before. Moyer, nevertheless, firmly believed she was culpable, and guilty of patricide and matricide, in his opinion because, Moyer says, Kara continually "lied through her teeth" during her questioning by the detectives.

"David," says Moyer, "gave detectives considerably more honest information. Detectives Tobin and Geesey had interrogated David first, so when Kara said, in front of her lawyer Bob Beyer and guardian, certain things [i.e., David's possession of guns when he arrived at the Borden home] the detectives quickly would challenge her by telling Kara that was not what David had said. Clearly then, she had to change her story a bit. Obviously, Kara didn't realize the information that Tobin and Geesey had from talking to David."

According to Moyer, Kara Borden was caught off balance by the fact that the investigators were aware of the three options that David had given her prior to coming over to her house: one, coming over to talk; two, coming over to get her; three, coming over to kill her parents.

There were other things that didn't square with what David told his interrogators and what Kara said. David had confessed that the two engaged in sex several times during their route out to Indiana. Kara had said they never had sex.

Moyer says, "it was those little things, along with the bigger things," that showed that one of the teenage lovers was a liar. Apparently it was Kara who was not telling the truth, says the ADA, because when confronted with the discrepancies, it was Kara who said she was mistaken.

To charge her, the prosecution had to show *probable cause* to meet the elements of a specific crime, and not just base it on the lying after the fact about something irrelevant. Moyer looked hard at whether Kara had aided or assisted Ludwig in any way in his escape from Lititz on November 13, 2005.

It seemed like he was responsible (and shouldered the blame) for everything. He threw the cell phones out of the car to avoid tracking. She didn't get the car or the money. She just went with him. Quite literally, she was along for the ride, if you were to believe them.

Moyer believes that Kara may have been experiencing a teenage angst common among girls her age, where they go through a stage of "hating" their parents. But, says the assistant district attorney, "You can't twist that angst into a crime whenever you see fit, unless you have the elements to ethically charge her." The Lancaster district attorney did not have any of those elements.

As to the notoriety of the case and the intense national focus it got, Susan Moyer says it was because of what the public gleaned from the over-hyped TV accounts of the story that dwelled on Kara's complicity, their religion, education and sexual activity. In actuality, they had little to do with the guilt or innocence of David Ludwig. It perplexed and upset people that seemingly upper-class, religious, homeschooled and intelligent people were involved in the sordid affair. The whole tragic case was an aberration.

Presently, says Moyer, there is civil litigation being pursued by the estate of the Borden family versus the Ludwig parents' insurance company. The plaintiffs are trying to subpoena the district attorney's records on the case, but there is a legal battle going on about this discovery phase. One thing that is certain: it will resurrect the story again in the public consciousness.

TWENTY-TWO

Graduation

On June 6, 2006, while awaiting trial, Ludwig received his high school diploma, along with six other inmates, during a modest commencement inside Lancaster County Prison. The imposing facility was a strange locale for such a ceremony. The forbidding-looking stone fortress had staged public hangings there up until 1912.

The county jail is located on the eastern side of Lancaster City, where it was constructed in 1852. The prison is actually touted in county and city tourist brochures and websites as a historic and architecturally interesting visitors' attraction. After seeing it, you can understand why. It was originally built in the style of a medieval castle, and retains much of that original appearance today.

Within its walls are housed 1,200 male and female inmates, which, according to Warden Vincent Guarini, is borderline overcrowded. The prison population is composed primarily of inmates from the age of 18 on up. Approximately 60 percent have not been tried or are awaiting some type of court action. The remaining 40 percent are sentenced to partial terms of imprisonment. A prisoner may be sentenced to any term of imprisonment in the county prison less than 5 years. Prisoners with maximums of 5 years or more must be sent, by law, to one of the twenty-seven prisons scattered democratically all over the state. As of June 6, the old castle-like fortress had been David Ludwig's home for seven months while he awaited his fast-approaching June 14 date in court.

Ludwig's parents, Gregory and Jane Ludwig, attended the ceremony, where prisoners and guests were feted with a luncheon. Warden Guarini attended, as did County Commissioner Dick Shellenberger, who made a brief speech, telling the new graduates, "Success is getting up one more time than you've fallen down."

Shellenberger also spoke with Ludwig privately and related to the media that he'd told David that, "God will be with you and that you need to continue to make right choices," adding that David responded with "a firm handshake."

Shellenberger also said Ludwig cried at times during the ceremony, and that he'd given Ludwig a tissue and also posed for a photograph with him. Gregory and Jane Ludwig took the podium, quoted Bible verses and spoke of the "importance of good choices."

Shellenberger commented that, "Mrs. Ludwig spoke very eloquently and praised her son."

Ted Zellers, who instructed Ludwig, said, "David is a very high achiever. He reached high academics in English, history and literature."

Zellers said that David had continued to be home-schooled, explaining that he'd received instruction from his parents while in jail: "David wrote his papers and mailed them to his mother for corrections. After she sent them back, he would rewrite them on a word processor.

"David is definitely college material," said Zellers, "and he is planning to enroll in college correspondence courses."

The proud parents, despite the venue, videotaped the event and took photos. Once the ceremony ended, the graduated inmates and their families spent some forty minutes together eating cake, sandwiches, potato chips, cheese and vegetables with dip.

"I told them to go back for seconds, thirds and fourths if they wanted, because the food was much better than what they normally get," Warden Guarini said, and added, "Today they weren't inmates; they were just kids."

By the tone of the response to the story on the graduation in the Lancaster *Intelligencer Journal*, one can assume that many in the community were outraged by the coddling tone of the event. The gushing newspaper story unleashed a torrent of letters to the editor, where readers expressed dismay at the ceremony, which they, as taxpayers, underwrote.

"Jodilynn" wrote:

getting his diploma & eating cake?
    the ludwigs should be very proud of him [sic]

Mrs mom5 expressed her outrage by writing:

Whatever happened to bread and water for those that take the lives of others?

This from "kepie":

no school, no parties,no tv, no email, or anything else,
Perhaps if we made jail bad the people wouldn't even think
about breaking the law again [sic]

"Hmac" was none too pleased either, writing:

We are worried about property taxes in this state, yet we
can waste money on educating someone who will be in
prison for life. [sic]

Warden Guarini said his star inmate's stay was un-
eventful, reporting that David Ludwig was very quiet,
kept to himself and caused no problems. The warden
does not term any prisoner a "model," but if he did,
David Ludwig would certainly qualify.

TWENTY-THREE

Guns, Sex and the Internet

Dr. Kathleen M. Heide, PhD, Professor of Criminology at the College of Arts and Sciences, University of South Florida, finds the case of David Ludwig to be a complicated one, a case that involves many critical adolescent issues. She knows from what she speaks; she is a nationally recognized expert on youth violence.

In the cases that Dr. Heide has actively investigated—and there have been many—when kids become enraged and there are weapons readily available, the risk of them committing a violent act is amplified; kids tend to be impulsive, she says.

Not surprisingly, the prosecution insisted the fact that Ludwig brought guns with him to the Borden house for the showdown that turned deadly proved premeditation. But that may not follow here, says the Florida psychotherapist. It goes back to the maturity of the brain. For an adult mind—at least 22 years of age—yes, it would suggest prior planning or premeditation, but not necessarily to the immature, impulsive type of mind. Taking the guns with him to the Bordens' home could have been done without David thinking of the magnitude, danger and implications of the act. It may have been part of his fantasy and something that he thought he could get away with. But, says Heide, without knowing his state of mind and studying his physiological report, it is too difficult to say. According to defense attorney Merrill Spahn, the release of that critical information is not going to happen, because that's the way David Ludwig insisted he wanted it.

District Attorney Donald Totaro has said that the number of guns found in the Ludwig residence—59—was not all that unusual in Lancaster County. Gun collecting and the popularity of hunting in the county is a long time-honored tradition among its citizens, and the DA says he sees no problem with that. Strangely, all the guns—minus the murder weapon—seized at the Ludwig home were eventually returned to Mr. Ludwig.

Lancaster County, of course, would seem to be a place where any mention of gun control by a politician would be a sure-fire way of guaranteeing defeat in any election, whether for dog catcher or district attorney. But at least one politician bucks that trend, Lancaster City Mayor Richard "Dick" Grey.

Mayor Grey is an outspoken proponent of stricter gun control laws in Pennsylvania. He is also an active member of New York Mayor Michael Bloomberg's task force Mayors Against Illegal Guns. The goal of the activist mayors is to draft federal legislation to slow the circulation of handguns in the United States. Mayor Grey clearly understands the problem, as he is also a former defense attorney and president of the Pennsylvania Association of Criminal Defense Attorneys. He has dealt with the consequences of handguns that fell into the hands of the wrong individuals. There is no doubt, as far as he is concerned, that a troubled teen like David Ludwig apparently was, should not have had easy access to handguns.

Grey, however, doesn't believe proliferation of handguns is unique to Lancaster County. He believes that the Commonwealth "is far too lax permitting the proliferation of guns to a degree that people who want to use them for illegal activities can easily do so." He also believes Pennsylvania's gun problems are the problems of its border states. He says with authority that in New York, a large percentage of the illegal guns used in crimes were purchased in Pennsylvania because it is so trouble-free.

One of the goals of the mayor is to make it into law that a resident of the state can "only" buy one handgun a month, thereby limiting a married couple to twenty-four handguns a year. The modest attempt at gun control has met with vehement resistance from gun-rights groups.

In December 2007 the bill to limit the number of guns was defeated by the legislature's judiciary committee in a bipartisan vote of 17–12 despite the lobbying of Governor Ed Rendell for its passage. Jake McGuigan, a spokesman for the National Shooting Sports Federation, said this about the bill's failure to pass muster in the committee:

Limiting the rights of the law-abiding is no way to reduce crime. Studies clearly demonstrate that one-gun-a-month laws don't work, and trying to pass legislation that will allow for local jurisdictions to place further restrictions on firearms

*and ammunition will only lead to thousands of
new gun-control laws and regulations that affect
law-abiding gun owners, none of which will reduce crime.*

Grey says that being a defense attorney for thirty-
five years has taught him that when someone breaks
into a house, the first thing they are looking for is
cash—then guns. They are stolen, he says, "because
they are easily marketable, or almost as good as cash."

Mayor Grey echoed Totaro in saying that the large
number of guns found in the Ludwig home doesn't surprise him. It leads him to question the whole sportsman
argument that the gun laws the state has are there to
protect the sportsmen's rights. Other than vintage guns,
Grey doesn't see any reason why a sportsman would
need so many:

"I don't know many people who go out hunting
with Glock pistols and semiautomatic assault rifles,
and if they are hunting, they are not hunting animals."

Grey would like to see appropriate measures in
place in the state so that sportsmen, people who want
to use guns for legitimate reasons and those who want
self-protection, have access to them, but that the number of guns and proliferation of them be limited so that
the rest of the public is protected, ". . . which is not the
case in Pennsylvania." Had the laws been in place, perhaps Michael and Cathryn Borden might still be alive.

Detective Chris Erb also thought David Ludwig's
easy access to such dangerous weaponry without being supervised was "beyond" him:

"I just don't understand how that can happen," Erb

said. "It really is an incomprehensible lack of good sense."

According to the Pennsylvania Department of Health, there were sixty-nine deaths and sixty-seven hospitalizations in Lancaster County in the two-year period of 2001–03—the latest years available—due to gunshot wounds. Besides the immeasurable and unquantifiable pain and suffering the deaths and injuries caused, the state found that the average cost of a hospitalization of a gunshot victim was $30,814. Most hospitalizations were paid for by taxpayers, since 72 percent of the victims were uninsured—amounting to $1,534,707 in Lancaster County for those two years.

Legislating the outright banning, or even just limiting the number of types of guns a citizen can purchase does not have even a remote chance of passing in the Keystone State. Gun-rights advocates point to a paper released in Boston discounting the relationship between gun ownership by citizens and elevated crime rates.

It was published in the *Harvard Journal of Law & Public Policy*, hardly a bastion of conservative thought. The paper, "Would Banning Firearms Reduce Murder and Suicide? A Review of International and Some Domestic Evidence," was impressively researched and presented by Don B. Kates (LLB Yale, 1966), an American criminologist and constitutional lawyer associated with the Pacific Research Institute, San Francisco, and Gary Mauser (PhD, University of California, Irvine, 1970), a Canadian criminologist and university professor at Simon Fraser University, Burnaby, BC, Canada.

The interesting thing about the report was that both researchers had expected the findings to be exactly the opposite. They wrote:

Whether gun availability is viewed as a cause or as a coincidence, the long term evidence is that gun ownership spread widely throughout societies consistently correlates with stable or declining murder rates.

Citing statistics the two researchers came to their startling conclusion:

The non-correlation between gun ownership and murder is reinforced by examination of statistics from larger numbers of nations across the developed world. Comparison of 'homicide and suicide mortality data for thirty-six nations (including the United States) for the period 1990–1995' to gun ownership levels showed 'no significant (at the 5% level) association between gun ownership levels and the total homicide rate.' Consistent with this is a later European study of data from 21 nations in which 'no significant correlations [of gun ownership levels] with total suicide or homicide rates were found.'

As a Pennsylvanian, Diane Edbril is concerned that the state is far too lax in tracking firearms sales and does not require residents to register them. The easy availability of guns lends itself to tragic situations where impulsive teenagers get to act out their anger and frustrations. That, Edbril says, is the case with David Ludwig.

Gun-owning citizens, Edbril says, have to be held accountable for their firearms. One law CeaseFire PA (the largest organization working to reduce gun violence) would like to see passed by the state legislature is that missing guns be reported by their owners. If that law had been in place in November of 2005, perhaps Mr. Ludwig's gun collection would have been properly stored; the missing guns might have been reported, and the deaths of Michael and Cathryn Borden might have been prevented.

The antiviolence organization would also like to see that large caches of firearms be monitored by police. It's a law, the group realizes, that has little chance of passing in the gun-loving state of Pennsylvania.

Katherine Ramsland holds graduate degrees in forensic psychology, clinical psychology, and philosophy. She teaches forensic psychology at DeSales University in Pennsylvania. Ramsland wrote extensively on the Borden murder case. On the subject of guns she wrote the following:

> *Since his father had plenty of guns, there's reason to believe that from this exposure Ludwig viewed weapons as a way to enforce his will. He was a hunter, so he understood the power of a gun. If he had fantasies that involved violence, it's likely that guns would have been part of them.*

Obviously, arguments can be made that the presence of so many guns in the Ludwig household greased David's descent into violence. Whether the availability of guns was an activator or a non-factor in the deaths of Michael and Cathryn Borden is debatable.

Many argued that by immersing David in the hunting culture he was being trained to be comfortable with killing. Believers of this theory say that animals often die slow, agonizing deaths. Sometimes death comes instantly with a perfectly aimed shot, but either way, they reason, a youth experiencing this death struggle becomes callused to the notion of death and dying. Proponents of this idea believe the leap from killing animals to humans becomes an easy one.

It is an "odd thing" about the hunting angle psychologically, Dr. Heide says, since there is a difference in deriving satisfaction from killing and torturing an animal as opposed to the desired challenge of a clean kill. To decipher the difference, a thorough psychotherapeutic analysis of the patient would have to be made.

Heide did do research in this area with a colleague, Linda Merz-Perez. The pair co-authored a study, "Animal Cruelty: Pathway to Violence Against People," on malevolent criminals who have shown a penchant for cruelty to animals while they were young. They studied violent offenders (murderers, rapists) versus non-violent offenders (drug dealers and thieves) at a maximum security prison. What they found was that the violent offenders were far more likely to have animal cruelty in their past than non-violent offenders.

But Dr. Heide cannot say categorically that hunting early in one's life is a predictor that the youth may be capable of killing humans as he matures. The only thing she could say about young hunters is that they may be more comfortable with the use of weapons and certainly more skilled at it. But suggesting that adolescents will be making the leap from hunting to homicide is just too much of a stretch for her.

The link between guns and religion was another hot topic of discussion in the case. It was reported that David's deeply religious father, besides building the bunker in his home, stocking it with provisions and maintaining a small arsenal of assorted firearms, was planning for the apocalypse as predicted in the Bible's Book of Revelations. Death, famine and plague dominate the scriptures in Revelations, but they also speak of the salvation of the faithful. Greg Ludwig, it seems, saw Y2K (year 2000) as the start of calamity and doom. Some speculated that that end-of-the-world kind of thinking was an inspiration to David to bring about his own "cataclysmic confrontation."

Because of David's father's doomsday beliefs, Dr. Heide thinks that maybe David was adversely affected, that he grew up in an atmosphere where the delusion of eminent death and destruction loomed. That might explain his use of violence to solve problems. His upbringing most likely imbued in him that the world was a violent and dangerous place, and one must act aggressively to survive.

Was David a psychopath? Legally, Heide speculates, he was. He exhibited a reckless behavior, an apparent lack of remorse, and had a cavalier attitude toward relationships with girls, where he used them, then discarded them. It clearly indicates, says the Florida psychologist, an antisocial attitude.

Another aspect of David's behavior drew interest. That was his unusual calmness and detached demeanor from the time he was captured till his court appearances. Under such duress, one would expect agitated or frightened behavior. It is possible, says Dr. Heide, that to be cool, calm and collected as a young person could suggest poor reality contact (often seen in someone with a psychotic disorder) or lack of a conscience, which is the hallmark of individuals often diagnosed with antisocial personality disorder if over 18.

When Dr. Heide, like many people, first heard of the case over the TV, she recalls wondering what Kara's involvement was, speculating that if she was even just a co-conspirator, then the case would be an interesting one of parricide. Though parricide (the killing of one's parent) turned out not to be the case legally, she found the murders fraught with juvenile issues of violence, sex and acculturation in a modern society.

Dr. Heide is careful to note that, since she never examined David Ludwig or Kara Borden, her observations are purely conjecture, but are based on her extensive knowledge of juvenile behavior and violence and what may have been the activators in the deaths of Michael and Cathryn Borden.

Being a firm believer that a human's brain is not fully developed until the age of 22–25 years, she considers David Ludwig, despite the law's view, to be an adolescent.

Knowing that adolescents do fantasize a lot, David "must have had destructive fantasies and was absorbed in violent thoughts." She considers such impulses not all that unusual, though it becomes an area of clinical concern when a youth spends quite a lot of time on them and starts acting on them.

Dr. Heide says there is usually a sense of unreality

in acting out a violent fantasy, and then suddenly, after the fact, there is the resulting shock of reality. Being immature, the juvenile is unable to process it, and as a result, becomes traumatized by it.

Kara's infatuation for David, and her not being able to process the reality of their situation, made going on the run with him a way of not dealing with the event. It was, in fact, a defense mechanism.

The Ludwigs, shortly after the murders, publicly expressed their "profound sorrow and shock." They, however, refused to discuss their religious beliefs with the press, except to say that the murderous actions of their son David "challenged everything about us."

The Roundtable on Religion & Social Welfare Policy, an Internet-based newsletter, is a good source of conservative thought "on policy and legal developments concerning the involvement of faith-based organizations in social services." On September 3, 2006, Helen Colwell Adams, a columnist for the newsletter, opined on the Borden murders as being the consequence of teen sex.

Adams wrote of a 9th grader with an older boyfriend who took issue with sexual abstinence advocate Pam Stenzel after she led a series of workshops in Lancaster County.

The girl wrote, Stenzel said, that Stenzel "was wrong to contend that ninth graders are too young to be dating." The girl said that "she could handle her relationship with an 18-year-old boyfriend who loved her."

The love-struck teen, Stenzel would later learn, was Kara Borden.

"Sex does have consequences," Stenzel argued.

"This case," she said, "extreme as it may have been, is one of them."

"Kids are inundated with media messages about extramarital sex," she said. "One result is that for people younger than 30, the average number of sexual partners now is 27.2."

"The media's really good at showing sex on a regular basis minus any type of consequences at all," she said.

Stenzel e-mailed back to Kara ". . . that what Kara thought didn't really matter: 'The fact that your parents have told you not to should carry some weight. Biblically, you have to listen to your parents. Your obligation is to honor them.' "

Another thing that had Stenzel shaking her head was learning that Kara Borden and David Ludwig spent a lot of time on MySpace and Xanga, where they maintained websites. Stenzel said this about those Internet services:

"A lot of kids are putting images of themselves out there that are not true. They think, 'In order to be cool, I have to put on my MySpace that I get drunk on a regular basis, that I have sex with multiple partners.' . . . How long does it go from 'we're talking about it' to actually participating in it?"

"That's not what's happening today," Stenzel said. Kids fall into two groups: those who aren't having sex, and "kids who are sexually active with multiple partners, completely indiscriminately. Hooking up, friends with benefits."

Parents, Stenzel says, have to educate and to set boundaries for their children. That's what Kara's parents were trying to do when they were murdered.

"Here were parents who were attempting to do a lot of things right," Stenzel said. ". . . You can do everything right as a parent . . . and your kid could still choose to do the wrong thing."

She tells parents they have to start building character in young children:

Delayed Gratification: "Sometimes we have to say no to something that might be nice in the short term" for something better in the long run.

Personal Responsibility: "If you do A, B is going to happen." And parents will not bail out the children when consequences are looming.

Empathy: "The ability to walk in someone else's shoes." Too many kids have "a complete lack of empathy. They are willing to hurt someone without regard. Because it's me, me, me."

On the religious issue in this case, the criminologist/psychologist Dr. Heide says that with strict religious upbringing, sometimes the rules are embraced, but not the underlying values. That is, making salvation more formulaic, like the rules in a game, as opposed to really endorsing it. An example, explained Dr. Heide, is "being pious in church and then leaving the parking lot and becoming a road rage monster." Being consistently moral, Heide has found, is often the big challenge in a young Fundamentalist's life.

A psychoanalytic assessment of Ludwig, says Heide, would probably discover whether he is or was delusional. Does he have an internalized value system—that is, does he have a conventional sense of what is right or wrong? Does he feel bad about killing the Bordens and take accountability for what he has done? Does he feel empathy, not only for the people he has killed, but also for the surviving victims—Kara and the other Borden children—whose lives he has altered forever?

As a psychopath, he might view the tragic incident as somebody else's fault—for instance, the murdered parents', who, if they hadn't prevented him from seeing Kara, wouldn't have been killed. He would be the victim then, since the Bordens had brought it on themselves.

A lot of kids use the Internet as a vehicle to express their destructive fantasies with websites and violent games. But when the adolescent becomes absorbed in destructive and violent images in what Dr. Heide calls "nihilistic thinking," then it becomes a real warning sign.

Heide says that as they begin to immerse themselves in the death-and-doom thinking, it becomes a more desirable thing to actually act out. In cases she has worked on as psychotherapist and criminologist, she has found that the magnitude of time involved in the absorption of violent thoughts and learning song lyrics—i.e. gangster rap—and doing little else, worries her.

The question Dr. Heide would have in a case like this—unless a severe mental illness was involved—would be: How could David profess strong moral values on one hand, but conduct nighttime home invasions and talk about killing people? "It just doesn't fit," she says.

Was the pious attitude something he just parroted because it was effective in gaining people's trust and respect? The crowd that he traveled in, the small, tight Christian community, would seem to magnify the importance of his purported religious bent.

Another crucial clue as to David Ludwig's low maturity level is the senselessness of the act, by which psychotherapists such as Dr. Heide mean that the murders didn't have to happen. There was no need to kill the parents; they did not physically threaten him, nor were they abusive prior to being shot. Yet somehow he justified it by convincing himself that they made him do it because they said no, he couldn't see their daughter, and their daughter was his, and nobody could take what was his away from him.

Treatment of this psychosis would involve bringing David to the point where he recognizes his personal responsibility for the misdeed and accepts the consequences of it. A therapist would then try to invoke some sense of remorse and empathy for his victims, which, says Heide, is very difficult to do. What's more is that if you fail, the prisoner/patient remains a very dangerous person, apt to commit the same kind of violence again and again. But David's first brush with the law, the statutory sexual assault of another young girl at his hunting cabin prior to his relationship with Kara, was a red flag that was ignored.

Perhaps the biggest concern is how the young of the community handle the tragic event of November 2005. The times being what they are, the best gauge of how they are dealing with it is to turn to the very outlet that

David and Kara used, the Internet. One friend wrote, in the shorthand of the medium:

people screw up, and do stupid things.

but david is a great guy a GREAT friend. and i refuse to hold this against him.

david is my friend.

granted i am very angry, and very VERY hurt, and at times didnt care what happened to him..deep down..i do care. i really do.

Another wrote sadly, but tersely getting to the bigger issue:

it's hard when someone you know is killed, it's even harder when someone you know kills someone . . ."

TWENTY-FOUR

Sentencing

It was on November 29, 2005, that District Attorney Don Totaro received an e-mail from David Ludwig's defense attorney Merrill Spahn that set David's fate on a course to resolution. Spahn proposed a meeting with the DA the next day where they could discuss options that the defense believed they had regarding the penalties Ludwig was facing for his crimes.

Totaro had a meeting scheduled with the designated trial judge about the case's progress, or lack of it, that morning at 8 AM. He replied by e-mail that he was available anytime after 8:30 AM. They met in his office on the fifth floor of the Lancaster County Courthouse. It was a relatively small legal community, and the attorneys all knew each other well. They had all squared off before the bench and argued their cases in front of juries. Each man was aware of the other's strengths and weaknesses, but would never share them with an outsider. Despite public perception, there is an honor among attorneys.

Spahn offered to waive the preliminary hearing scheduled for December 16 and agreed to amending the complaint to contain the additional charges of statutory sexual assault and the Uniform Firearms Act (UFA) charges if the DA would remove the kidnapping charge from the complaint. That was fine with Totaro, since they had already decided they would drop the kidnapping charge. At this time they were still unsure if Kara could be charged for any complicity in the murders, but that was another matter that did not concern Ludwig's defense. That would be in the capable hands of defense counsel Bob Beyer.

Spahn also requested copies of David's statements to police, autopsy reports and a copy of the report by the first responding police officer on the scene at the Borden residence. At the meeting, defense attorney Spahn also intimated that his client might be amenable to a plea of guilty to first-degree murder in exchange for a sentence of life in prison, rather than death. The defense counsel knew Totaro would file for the death sentence anyway for procedural reasons, but wanted to start the negotiation process on the inevitable penalty phase. The purpose for the defense requests was to have everything on the record, which made evidence challenges more procedural.

In a hearing, the first responding officer would describe the situation he'd seen when he arrived. The detectives who took the statements of the defendant would also be called and they would read the statements verbatim into the record and to the district judge. Following the detectives, the forensic pathologist who performed the autopsies on the victims would establish the causes and the manners of death. This all had to be done for the DA to convince the district judge to have the case returned to the Common Pleas Court for a trial.

The defense had a good reason for not seeking an open hearing on the charges against their client. The last thing they wanted to have happen was to hear the detective read Ludwig's incriminating statement. It would have been shocking to the public and perhaps damaging, and certainly fodder for the story-hungry press. If the hearing were held the next day, it would be in all the media reports, prejudicing the public against Ludwig and potentially tainting the jury pool.

Later that day Totaro met with his office's director of the Victim/Witness Services, Pamela Grosh, and related to her the latest developments so she could apprise the Borden family members of what had been transpiring.

On December 2, Totaro received an e-mail from defense attorney James Gratton, who, after speaking with their client, agreed to the additional charges while dropping the kidnapping charge.

Totaro spoke with the Bordens' eldest sons, Justin and James, on December 6, when he explained to them personally what was going on in negotiations with Ludwig's defense. He told the two young men that, despite the offer being made by the other side, he still intended to file the notice that the prosecution would seek the death penalty for procedural reasons. A conference call was set up for December 15 where all the family members scattered about the country would be included.

In the conference call, which lasted about an hour, Totaro laid out all the options: the waiver, the preliminary hearing, the first-degree murder proposal, the death penalty and all conceivable scenarios that might arise. The preliminary hearing was the next day, and a decision on the waiver was needed then. The DA had explained to them that if they had the hearing, he would have to produce the statements that the defense was requesting. The prosecution essentially was not giving up anything that the defense was entitled to at a hearing anyway, but they were allowing the defense to spare themselves from publicly airing David's confession.

For the next several months, from a court-outlined schedule, the DA's office had to provide all police reports and discovery evidence to the defense attorneys. It took a while, since the DA's office would eventually compile over two thousand pages of reports and interviews, then organize them, before turning over a copy to the defense.

Two more scheduled arraignments, on January 24 and February 1, were waived by the defense.

By early February 2006, the DA's office was waiting patiently while the defense pored over the mountain of paperwork to see if they had grounds for suppression of evidence for such procedural faux pas as an illegal search and seizure, or a Miranda violation. The date for the suppression of evidence was March 30; the trial was set for June 14.

Apparently the defense believed it needed more time to study the prosecution's evidence and to formulate its strategy. After a Motion for Extension of Time, the March date was moved back to April 26 and then again, after another motion, to May 15.

Totaro says that at no time did defense get back to him to say that Ludwig was rethinking his guilty plea. Totaro proceeded as if he would have to argue the case in front of a jury.

On May 8 Totaro spoke with the extended Borden

family one more time over the conference call line. The DA wanted to be sure the victims' extended family was all on the same page about how he was to prosecute David Ludwig.

Justin and James Borden basically wanted a guarantee of conviction on first-degree murder and a life sentence without the possibility of parole. The rest of the family adopted that viewpoint on punishment, no doubt out of deference to the two oldest children of Michael and Cathryn Borden.

The family was well aware that if they permitted the case to go to trial, they risked not only a lighter sentence, but also the possibility of appeals that could go on for more than twenty years. They wanted the nightmare to end. All agreed to the waiver and taking death off the table.

One thing the family was insistent on was that the murderer not profit in any way from his crimes. Totaro was in agreement and made sure that language, in no uncertain terms, was written into the guilty plea agreement.

Totaro also wanted the sentences for all the crimes (homicides, statutory sexual assault, reckless endangerment and the Uniform Firearms Act) to run consecutively. The tough-talking DA did not want to minimize one life over another, or lessen the seriousness of any of the additional counts by running those sentences concurrently. The penalties had to be the maximum that could be imposed under Pennsylvania law for those counts. No one on the conference call uttered a dissenting voice.

On May 16 the defense was granted its motion for yet another time extension to file any necessary pre-trial motions and/or preliminary death penalty motions until Monday, June12. The hearing never took place. The opposing sides were in agreement on charges and sentences, so it was unnecessary. If there were no surprise developments, the June 14 hearing would just be a walk-through.

On that late spring morning, all was ready to be presented to Judge David Ashworth in Courtroom #3, on the third floor of the Lancaster County Courthouse. But as Don Totaro said, "You never know how these things will turn out."

The DA knew from first-hand experience that the defendant could change his mind at the last second and insist on entering an innocent plea or a guilty plea to a lesser charge. That, of course, was his right.

Judge Ashworth had been on the bench since 2000. Prior to becoming a judge, he was in private practice, specializing in civil litigation. In his early 50s, Ashworth is a widely respected judge in Lancaster County legal circles, and considered to be neither pro-prosecution nor pro-defense.

Prior to his appearance in court, in his holding cell, David had to fill out a seven-page form that asked some basic questions about himself, if he understood his rights and if he was of sound and sober mind. In his distinctive and legible scrawl he signed his life away to the Commonwealth of Pennsylvania. David Ludwig, 19 years of age, would spend the rest of his young life behind bars.

The courtroom was packed with the curious and the media. The media was a little less of a presence, since the prospect of a dramatic long-drawn-out trial was now highly unlikely. Cameras and recording devices are not permitted in Pennsylvania courtrooms.

Totaro stood at a sidebar next to the judge, and David Ludwig stood at the defense's table flanked by his two lawyers, James Gratton and Merrill Spahn. Ludwig did not engage in any conversations with his legal representatives, just a hushed whisper or two now and then.

David's paperwork was given to Totaro, who read it aloud in court.

A detailed, lengthy colloquy ensued where David was asked if he understood the terms of the plea and sentencing, and was in agreement with them. The judge's job is to observe and listen, making sure the defendant is cogent and knows his constitutional rights, and comprehends what he is being charged with.

Ludwig answered all the questions properly, and was convincing in his affirmative replies in understanding his rights and the sentences.

Since the sentences agreed upon by the defense and the state were the maximum allowed, there was little chance they would be altered by Judge Ashworth, a conservative jurist when it came to punishment.

After Ashworth accepted the pleas, he formally sentenced the young man standing in front of him to a grand total of two life terms without parole plus an additional 9½ to 19 years for the reckless endangerment, weapons and statutory sexual assault charges. Ludwig was also assessed $125,515.82 in restitution ($619.62 of the total was assessed court fees).

The judge advised Ludwig of his appeal rights, and then it was over. The hearing had lasted forty-five minutes. There were no surprises. David Ludwig was then led out of the courtroom in handcuffs and returned to his cell in the Lancaster County jail. On June 20, 2006, at 10:19 AM, Ludwig was transported by the Lancaster Sheriff's Department from Lancaster County jail, 90 miles to the State Correctional Institution in Camp Hill. SCI Camp Hill serves as the state's diagnostic and classification center for men, and it was there that the Department of Corrections (DOC) would decide which state prison David Ludwig would be housed at for the foreseeable future.

One reason the sitting DA was so adamant about paying close attention to the finer points of the law was that he feared a couple years down the road, after Ludwig had been absorbed into the prison community, he might change his mind about his legal standing, and file an appeal—which is, of course, his right. Rarely, in these circumstances, do the defendant's original attorneys file them. It is the "jailhouse lawyers," fellow prisoners, who concern any district attorney. These self-educated busybodies were sure to tell Ludwig that his "outside" lawyers were incompetent, that there were things they should have done and that he'd been "railroaded."

"The next thing you know," says Totaro, "is, you got an appeal being filed basing their claims that the defendant's counsel was receiving ineffective service of counsel. This is what I was trying to protect all [the Borden family, the DA's office] from." As of this writing, two years after his incarceration, David Ludwig has had no appeals filed on his behalf.

TWENTY-FIVE

Faith

Besides homeschooling, Fundamental Christian belief was an issue in the case that was continually raised and discussed in the media. Lancaster County—besides its famous Amish, Mennonite and Moravian faiths—is home to some 700 Christian congregations. The Lititz Christian Church is one such congregation.

The business card of Thomas P. Gotwalt speaks volumes. Besides simple religious imagery that depicts what appears to be a chalice, under Gotwalt's name is the congregation's name and address. Gotwalt bestows no title on himself, and the address is his home. There is no steepled, brick-and-mortar church, no national affiliation. It's the simplicity that strikes you. Perhaps that is because Tom Gotwalt is a simple man of faith, with no airs, yet blessed with an impressive intellect.

He is no fire-and-brimstone evangelist. He speaks softly and thoughtfully. His strong faith in his God, Jesus Christ, is what impresses. Tom Gotwalt volunteered to accompany David Ludwig's confused and distraught parents to the police interview on that nightmarish day in November 2005.

There are only 150 active members in the Lititz

Christian Church. The congregation usually meets on Sundays at the Lititz Community Center. An outsider cannot help but wonder how the 53-year-old, bespectacled Gotwalt, a husband, father of four and a home mortgage holder, survives in the secular world. When asked, Gotwalt quietly smiles and simply says his flock, albeit a small one, has been "loving" in the support of their religious leader.

The smile disappears when the subject changes from church and community life to the events of November 13, 2005. It was a tragic incident that still has the small-town pastor pondering the sense of it all. Then there was the national media attention.

"We have been pursued by every known life-form regarding this situation," Gotwalt says of the media hordes that the Ludwig family and their faith advisor found themselves hounded by since the morning of November 13. Fed up and disillusioned with the pursuing newspeople, the interview he granted to this author would be his one and only.

Gotwalt explained that he and the Ludwigs are not dealing with a cut-and-dried issue: "There is no logic in a catastrophe," Gotwalt said. "At best it is somewhat chaos theory management. And the mathematics behind chaos theory is diverse, diffuse and not easy. When it comes to people and what's involved in what is variously known as the heart of man, there is a tremendous spectrum and a varied ability in response curves, not just in how people respond, but when they respond."

Furthermore, he says, some of the people close to David Ludwig, even now, have not completely processed all that has happened, somewhat like shell-shocked soldiers. This is why Gotwalt is very cautious about what it is he should say about the tragedy. He is reticent to give facts or a lot of details, because the book is not closed in his calling to serve those who are still deeply grieved over this situation. Even though the public may want the story, Gotwalt offers no apologies to them for his keeping mum on the subject, because his duty, as he sees it, is to those in need and not in satisfying the public curiosity.

He said that since the events of two years ago, David's parents, Greg and Jane Ludwig, are no longer members of the Lititz Christian Church. He would not disclose the reasons why they left.

Born, raised and educated in Lancaster County, Gotwalt describes his church as a "small, Biblically based Christian community that simply takes the Bible at face value and holds it as doctrinally correct, pure and able to guide us."

"We are very orthodox in our practice in many ways," said Gotwalt. Like most traditional Christian faiths, Lititz Christian meets on Sunday.

Basically—and no doubt oversimplifying a complex issue—there are two models for churches, one being the kind that is based on programs and the other that is based on relationships. They can merge, and often do, to accomplish some wonderful things, but the Lititz Christian Church definitely comes down on the side of relational-based faith. The small church does not have a liturgy like their Roman Catholic or Lutheran (the church Gotwalt was brought up in) brethren. Members do declare that they are absolutely in need of the grace of God, either through song or testimony. There is worship and instruction through sermons.

Although the Lititz Christian Church is not a part

of a larger umbrella group, they shy away from calling themselves "an independent church," something Gotwalt says has gotten a bad rap. It's been perceived that being independent has potential for swinging off good solid footing and chasing after some narrow doctrine. The church is led by a plurality of elders, of which Gotwalt is one. Their church is a dynamic one and has no list of do's and don'ts. They are simple in their address of behavior, and find great strength and resolve in the keeping of Biblical principles.

Gotwalt explains his life work as a calling. "The call[ing] is ultimately subjective, yet thoroughly convincing."

The congregation does not have the sense of being protected or belonging to a larger entity, such as mainstream denominations, yet Gotwalt says there is a sense of being part of a dynamic that is worldwide.

The Lititz Christian Church has no affiliation with any homeschooling network, but Gotwalt fully supports the concept, referring to taking on the burden of homeschooling as a "calling" as well. Gotwalt and his wife homeschooled just two of their own four, and that was for just one primary school year.

In Lancaster County the homeschooling network is so well-developed, and encompasses so many people from different churches, that there is an understandable overlap between the network and the church communities. No single church is tagged as *the* homeschooling church over another. A large percentage of his church's congregation is homeschooled, but it is neither encouraged nor discouraged, he says.

The Ludwigs showed interest in the church years ago and began to "fellowship" with them. Gotwalt would not talk about their relationship, or, for that matter, any other church-related relationship—Sam Lohr and his family were also church adherents—because it is personal. He would say that the Ludwigs are wonderful people and he "loves them dearly."

On Sunday morning, November 13, the police notified Gotwalt, through channels, of the transpiring events over on Royal Drive. Gotwalt's colleague, Mike Shelley, had relationships in the Warwick Township Police Department and was a friend of Chief Garipoli, hence the courtesy. Although he wouldn't confirm it, the two churchmen must have learned in conversations with police that they were looking for one of their church members, David Ludwig. Gotwalt and Shelley were "invited into the mobile command center" by the police.

Both men had been in many difficult circumstances as a pastoral team, and made the effort to facilitate whatever they could for those in need, and the police. In catastrophic response, there are people who are trained for it, and Gotwalt and Shelley were there, in his words, "simply to serve."

The Bordens were not members of Gotwalt's church, so consequently he did not know them. Gotwalt, of course, did know David Ludwig. When asked how well, his answer was, "I guess not well enough." He would say he knew prior to November 13 that David was troubled. "He was an active member of the church and he was struggling," Gotwalt explained.

There was no signal of David's impending rampage. His apparent struggles with parental authority were triggering deepening concern. Any propensity for violence would have been purely speculative on anyone's part.

While situated at the police command post a block away from the Borden residence, Gotwalt learned that Greg and Jane Ludwig would be brought over from their home in Lititz a few miles away.

"Obviously, in the shock they were in," said Gotwalt, "it would be preferential to have somebody known to intercept them and help them in that moment. That was me."

The day, says Gotwalt, seemed three years long. Never had anyone in the community seen such a massive police presence. SWAT team members were belly-crawling through the shrubbery; helicopters circled overhead and police squad cars with lights flashing blocked roads. The Ludwig couple spoke little.

"To know that your son," says Gotwalt, "is involved—you are not going to be standing around talking about your hopes."

Gotwalt attended to the Ludwigs for hours so that their "blood pressure did not go over the edge." He sat in the back of an ambulance with the frightened pair because it was the only quiet and removed place they could find.

Once they were brought over to the Warwick Township Police Department, Gotwalt, too, was asked to be interviewed there. He surmised it was part of the police protocol and cooperated with them fully. Because of the pumping adrenaline, there was a time warp for Gotwalt. He can't remember if the interview lasted twenty minutes or an hour. Time-wise, all he can recall was that it was late afternoon by the time he accompanied Greg and Jane Ludwig home.

In the ensuing days, Gotwalt was at their beck and

call to advise and comfort. He would not divulge any of what was said or done.

He would say that all he tried to do was create a loving atmosphere, because "such an atmosphere is the only one where something better can happen."

Despite some reports, Gotwalt claims he did not turn in one of the tossed-out cell phones belonging to the wanted fugitives. "Urban legend," he says.

Later, when asked, Lieutenant Ed Tobin confirmed this revelation. It was not the Lititz church pastor, but David's friend Kayla Jeffries.

Gotwalt knew of David's previous incident with a young girl at the hunting cabin, but does not know a lot of details. Contrary to rumor and written reports, Gotwalt firmly asserts that his church had no part in any consultation or meetings between the two families on how the incident would be dealt with. "No minister," said the Lititz pastor, "moderated, as far as I know, any planned meetings between the two families."

Gotwalt found the media attention offensive but understandable.

"We are curious creatures," he explained, "and tend to love resolution even when we can't have it, so in the absence of clear resolution, we invent it. We must connect dots."

The real annoyance for Gotwalt was the intrusive nature of the newspeople. In situations like these, it is for the media to give the involved families time to figure out which way is up. But given the age we live in, says the spiritual leader, and the ability to dispense information, they did—much of it false. Gotwalt says the family and friends of David Ludwig were "quoted and quoted, but mostly misquoted." In lieu of good data, he believes, they start "slinging things," and these things become accepted as fact before ever being investigated. All this has given the former pastor to the Ludwigs reason not to sit down with the media to discuss the case.

Gotwalt says he was, and still is, a friend of David Ludwig, and is not ashamed of it. They exchange letters frequently.

But getting answers as to why the murders happened would be fruitless, the pastor says. By attempting that, you would be looking for a cause of the effect. Gotwalt defers to the Bible when asked about this psychological aspect and if it can provide answers about David's motives: "The mind, which is linked to the heart, is indiscernible to mankind."

It is a vain attempt, he explains, to try to find the cause for the effect, when the effect is what our present society ignores: the three-letter word "sin." Only God can discern it, but with his help, mankind can conquer "this desperately wicked heart."

"Subscribers to humanism think man to be inherently good," says Gotwalt, and that we simply need to find out why we made a mistake, whereas in Gotwalt's Christian world, it is believed that man was born in sin, but that he can be restored with God's help.

David Ludwig, says his former pastor, is not a product of society's moral decay, but a product of his own personal life, like all of us. David Ludwig is not unique.

TWENTY-SIX

SCI Pine Grove

SCI Pine Grove is located in Indiana County, south-western Pennsylvania, approximately 60 miles north-east of Pittsburgh and 218 miles west of Lancaster. It is a maximum-security prison especially built for male juvenile felons or, as the Pennsylvania Department of Corrections (DOC) calls them, Young Adult Offenders (YAOs).

The Commonwealth is a pioneer in the development of programs that deal with the growing problems of juvenile crime and punishment. One of the answers their DOC came up with was SCI Pine Grove and its Young Adult Offender Program (YAOP).

The YAOP is primarily designed for those offenders between the ages of 15 and 20 who were tried and sentenced as adults due to the nature of their crimes. David Ludwig was confined with approximately 300 other YAO inmates on August 8, 2006, when he was transferred to the state-of-the-art facility from SCI Camp Hill.

The institution that will be Ludwig's home for the foreseeable future was the fruit of legislation signed by Republican Governor Tom Ridge, who was committed to a strong law and order platform. Ridge later was appointed the first Secretary of Homeland Security by President George W. Bush after 9/11, based on his solid credentials as a tough foe on crime.

In 1995, Ridge called the General Assembly into special session to consider, according to the Pennsylvania Historical and Museum Commission, a series of crime-fighting measures.

"As a result of the session," says the Commission's biography, "Ridge signed over forty new anti-crime laws mandating restitution to crime victims, creating a state-level crime victim's advocate office, establishing a DNA database for monitoring sex offenders, a 'three-strikes' law for repeat offenders, and increased penalties for murder convictions."

There also was consideration given to the growing juvenile crime problem.

Governor Ridge was a firm believer that, no matter what the age, "if you do the crime, you do the time." The problem was, the state had no place to put juvenile offenders without integrating them into the older institution-hardened prison population.

YAOs, upon conviction in juvenile courts, used to be turned over to the Department of Public Welfare (separate from the DOC) where they were housed in their institutions until they reached 21 years of age, at which time they were released. This scenario was the problem that Governor Ridge's legislative initiative hoped to solve—keeping dangerous YAOs off the street until they were rehabilitated and had served the adult time.

Common sense won out when it was decided to build a secure prison just for the juveniles where hopefully they could be rehabilitated. Two years from its inception, Pine Grove opened in February 2002. Today all the young offenders in the state who are sentenced as adults are imprisoned at Pine Grove.

But make no mistake about it: Pine Grove is a high-security prison housing armed robbers, rapists and murderers. Superintendent Joe Mazurkiewicz says the prison staff controls the lives of the inmates twenty-four hours a day, whether in therapy or in classes, earning a GED, or even a college degree. Outside the classroom, inmates are either engaged in a structured recreation period or locked up in their cells, usually on average eighteen hours a day.

Pine Grove's twenty-three acres are fenced, and armed with cameras and auto alarm detection sensors. Inmates are also monitored by camera surveillance 24/7 and eyeballed by approximately 200 guards. Pine Grove is what the state calls a custody level 4 institution—one step below a level 5, or the highest maximum-security prison. Mazurkiewicz is quick to point out that Pine Grove is capable of keeping maximum-security prisoners, and does. Due to chronic overcrowding in all the other state prisons, 400 of the beds not taken by YAOs are filled by adult inmates in separate buildings.

"If there is a breach of security," says Mazurkiewicz, "we act in an appropriate and quick manner. We try not to let them get to the point where they would even attempt to escape from the facility." In its six-year history there has never been a successful escape from Pine Grove.

YAO inmates are "cell-housed," two to a cell, in two buildings. Each building has two wings; each wing is divided into three pods. Meals are served in a dining hall that inmates walk to under guard escort, and the dining times are coordinated so the YAOs don't eat with the 400 adult prisoners. Privileges to use the chapel, gym or yard are structured strictly so that every minute of the inmate's day is accounted for. Because most of the YAOs come from dysfunctional families and backgrounds, a higher level of structure is needed here than in other Pennsylvania state prisons.

The YAOP is built on the concept of a therapeutic community, designed to use behavior modification as a primary management tool. Inmates, under the guidance of staff, encourage other inmates to correct their behavior and thinking so that they can be more productive in either society or other institutions.

The YAOP starts off with the Leadership Development Program (LDP) which is an all-consuming ninety-day combination of an orientation program and a boot camp regimen. The LDP's goal is to instill a sense of discipline and self-respect. In the early phases, an inmate attends very broad programs that build upon one another. In the later phases, the treatment changes to a more focused and intensive treatment plan based upon the needs of the individual offender. Specific programs target sex offenders, drug and alcohol abuse, anger management and other problematic behavior.

The inmates meet several times a day and only associate with fellow members on similar levels of programming needs. According to Mazurkiewicz, "The inmates eat, sleep and breathe the Young Adult Offender Program." They can earn the "privilege" of working a job when they complete their educational needs. "But," says, the warden, "their main job is to go to school and finish the program."

Hands-on training is provided, allowing the YAOs to develop employable job skills depending upon their aptitude. Programs offered include building maintenance, AutoCAD drafting, culinary arts and business education.

Corrections counselors, psychologists, drug and alcohol treatment specialists, school teachers, doctors and dentists make up a full third of the prison staff. The healthcare professionals are a particularly busy lot, since many of the inmates come from an impoverished background where hygiene was not good. Not surprisingly, Pine Grove is the most expensive prison per inmate to operate in the Commonwealth.

Inmates who successfully complete the program are given the option to remain at Pine Grove or transfer to other institutions that better suit them. Often the inmate wants to be moved to another prison that is closer to home, so family and friends can visit more frequently. Mazurkiewicz, however, says that it is common for the young inmates to opt to stay, since they know they are in a safe secure facility, they know the system and the staff, and have made friends with other prisoners. Many of the YAOs "graduate" to the adult side and can stay and continue with their education and therapy while serving out their sentences.

Lifers like David Ludwig are given the option to stay as well, on a case-by-case basis, says the superintendent. If the inmate completes the program successfully he can also opt to stay at Pine Grove. Those who fail are transferred to a prison that DOC determines is the most secure for the inmate. Demographically, Pine Grove has the youngest inmate population in the Commonwealth.

A question arises that begs for an answer concerning the "rehabilitation" of David Ludwig, that is: What's the point, since he will never be freed? Superintendent Mazurkiewicz is quick to answer:

"These inmates are still people, no matter what they have done. Even if they are not going to be paroled, they need to be better citizens in jail, and as productive as society will allow them to be under the circumstances. 'Rehabilitated' prisoners, to use your choice of words, are more manageable than ones that are not."

Pine Grove follows the same guidelines for visitation rights as the rest of the DOC system uses; that is, inmates can place individuals on their list and they are free to visit Friday–Monday, 8:30 AM–3:30 PM. Each inmate is limited to four visits a month in an open communal area. Legal and spiritual counselor visits do not count against their limits. Problem inmates can see only immediate family members, but in a "non-contact area," where they speak on a phone and are separated by glass.

Ludwig has become exactly the model inmate his defense attorney Merrill Spahn had predicted he would be. David was head of the student council of youths who still were studying to graduate with a GED. He has planned fund-raisers for charities near where he is incarcerated and has counseled other inmates.

Unlike with most inmates he has represented, Spahn has kept in contact with David Ludwig. He reports that David has had a hard time coming to terms with what he did and how he shattered the lives of so many. It has also been difficult accepting the fact that he is never getting out of prison. He, however, remains firm in his religious beliefs, and his former defense attorney is sure that David will someday serve in some kind of pastoral, ministerial or counseling capacity in prison.

Samuel Lohr, David's best buddy and cohort on the "night patrols," has not had any communication with David since November 12, 2005, the night before the murders. He has not visited him in prison, written any letters or spoken to him over the phone. It's not because he doesn't want to. He figures that, just three years after the murders, it's simply not a good idea. He adds that he wants to re-establish communications with him in the future when the time is right. David Ludwig, after all, is still his friend.

"Being a felon myself now," says Lohr, referring to the convictions for his and Ludwig's night patrols, "it is not a good idea to correspond, and it is illegal for me to visit him. It's safer not to talk to him for what people would say."

Sam says the tragedy of it all does not hang over his head now. He has pretty much put it behind him, even though a day doesn't pass when he doesn't think about it and his friend David.

"Now looking back at it," says Lohr, "I see it as something that was kind of a blessing for me, because it woke me up a lot. I realized that I can't be stupid. I really got to get a hold of who I am and have to become somebody that thinks that the way I was wasn't cool or safe. In a lot of ways it has given me the moral boundaries that I didn't have then."

Why David killed the Bordens is the "biggest mystery" to Sam. He remembers asking David once on one of their night patrols to Kara's house what they would do if they got caught. He told David he was going to "drop and roll and run," but David replied coldly, "I'd shoot them."

Sam laughed it off at the time, figuring it was something kids would say jokingly. But it's not something that he takes lightly anymore, after someone who'd said it to him later went ahead and did it.

Pondering the reason David killed the Bordens, Sam does not think it was out of love for Kara. He had been getting what he wanted from her, and as long as he was not caught doing it, everything was okay. But having been caught with two previous girlfriends already, and having run away with one of them, he was now prepared for any kind of conflict, as was ingrained in him by his father the survivalist. As Sam put it, "when it came down to getting caught again, he wasn't willing to get caught again."

Sam Lohr had been waiting for his day in court since February '06, after being released on $15,000 unsecured bail when his attorney convinced District Judge Daniel Garrett that Sam wasn't a flight risk.

On December 22, 2006, Lohr (a 2005 graduate of the Mason Dixon Homeschoolers Association) pleaded guilty to criminal trespass of the Ambrose home, and two counts of firearms carried without a license, during a brief hearing before Lancaster County Judge David L. Ashworth. There was no agreement on a sentence between Assistant District Attorney K. Kenneth Brown and Lohr's attorney, Janice Longer. Lohr and Longer only spoke in response to questions from Ashworth. Fellow participant Alita Stoner, who was

16 at the time they broke into the home, had not been charged.

The Ambrose family, like the Lohrs, were members of the Lititz Christian Church, and spoke to the judge on Sam's behalf for leniency. Samuel Lohr received no jail time, but got seven years' probation, which allowed him to continue his college education uninterrupted in Florida. The 19-year-old breathed a sigh of relief upon hearing his fate.

One wonders if he had thought of his best friend David, sitting in a maximum security prison for the rest of his life, and if he thanked God that he wasn't with him.

Epilogue

Kayla Jeffries no longer attends church. She credits the "issues" she had with the congregation's adults as a result of the murders of the Bordens that made her "drift away" from her faith. Kayla confesses that it was a general disillusionment that was a fallout of the tragic events of November 13, 2005, that also led to the break. She doesn't like to discuss it, for she feels it is private.

Detective Ed Tobin, who interviewed Kayla three or four times during the course of the investigation and got to know her family well, called Kayla "our go-to girl" when they needed confirmation on various pieces of information about David. Tobin said she was "a typical kid" who was "a little skeptical of adults." Kayla, he says, doesn't relish being the "go-to girl" for David and Kara.

The fact that Kayla and David still regularly communicate shows the Warwick Township detective that Kayla "has yet to grasp the whole concept of David having committed such a horrific act." But Kayla has her reasons.

Kayla went to the funeral of the Bordens and "cried a lot." She spoke to Kara and Katelyn briefly and gave her condolences. She would be there for Kara for weeks after her parents' murders, though they never spoke about "it." But their conversations grew more distant and infrequent as time went by, until they abruptly ended when Kara went to live with relatives in another part of the Commonwealth. It was something that she said she had no control of, alluding to adults as being the reason the two good friends stopped communicating. Kayla expressed herself in the following poem she wrote:

No Matter What

Not quite three months ago
A tragedy occured
Forever changing lives
Anger it stirred

Causing the never ending change
And endless pain
Mistakes have been made
Yourself forever you will blame

Others knew your secret
but didn't say a word
Empty confused eyes
Your cries cannot be heard

You're so far away
in my heart you'll always be
Always on my mind
My love i hope you see

We may not be together now
However our hearts are mended
and the strength of our friendship
I never doubt will be bended

2-6-06

Now a 20-year-old young adult, and three years distant from that horrible day, she still talks to David, who has limited access to a phone in prison. They also exchange letters. David, she says, is doing "okay" and has adjusted to prison life. Because Ludwig would not talk about his life behind bars, she would not either, preferring to honor his wishes not to divulge details about his incarceration.

Sam and Kayla have talked only a couple of times since the murders. Kayla has mixed feelings about him because he "pretty much blamed everything on David" when he was in court for entering the Ambroses' home. In Kayla's opinion he twisted what happened a lot to make himself appear less guilty in court than he was.

The Sam she knew and loved was funny, honest, adventurous and determined to succeed at whatever he did. Sam, she said, would always help a friend in need, any way he could.

David, Kara, Sam and Kayla would watch movies together. They went to the fair together, where they would meet up with other friends and hang out. They often went driving aimlessly around, as most kids their age did. Sam always made her laugh with his goofy imitations and jokes. But now all Kayla has to say about him is, "through all this, people's true colors have shown."

Kayla, unashamedly, has remained loyal to David.

She believes there will never be an explanation for the terrible thing he did. She says it was not the David she knew.

Kayla says that perhaps the killing of the Bordens was an act of desperation on David's part, for fear of losing Kara forever. Nevertheless, she says, she doesn't regret the friendship the three of them had, recalling how they hardly ever argued about anything and how there was never a dull moment with them. She claims they were "three of the most laid-back kids" she knew, while wondering aloud, ". . . if that made sense in light of what happened?" Kayla confessed that she missed them more and more every day, but holds out little hope the three can be together again.

She visited David on her twentieth birthday in the beginning of February 2008. It was the first time she'd seen him in person since the Thursday before November 13, 2005. It was a "good visit," she says.

"We just talked and caught up and played a game," Kayla related. "It was very emotional leaving . . . David doesn't show emotions publicly, but if you know him you can read his face and know what he's feeling. And that's what made it harder to visit him, cuz I know we just both wanted to cry. Seeing him for the first time in over two years was very emotional. Needless to say it was a quiet ride home."

Kayla wrote the following thoughts to the author in an e-mail:

They really are my best friends [David & Kara]. Even though I am unable to see or talk to Kara, i think about her everyday. I have many pictures in my room of her and i. I hope one day we are able to talk and hopefully be friends again. But as for now, it's just waiting and hoping. As far as David, I've known him since what feels like forever. Yes, he screwed up big time and I know that, as does he and he regrets it . . . but i still love him and care about him. It seemed so easy for everyone to turn their backs on him and abandon him, then it did for them to stick by him. Bottom line, he messed up but i still love him and miss him everyday. I love both of them and miss them everyday. They were a huge part of my life. And what happened is tragic, but none can change it. What's done is done and as much as it breaks my heart to think about that day, I can't help but wonder, Why us? Why Lititz, Pennsylvania? Why David? Why Kara? Why Mr. & Mrs. Borden. There are so many questions that go through my mind everyday, every other day, every week . . . that i honestly don't ever think will be answered. And maybe, just maybe it's for the best. I still feel like I'm in a dream that I can't seem to wake up from!

It's a nightmare that Lancaster County will not soon forget.